Mike Frost is one of the sharpest think[...] mean that he's clever (he is), but that h[...] nonsense with prophetic clarity. And so, of course, this book does just that. Large swaths of the Western church are in dire danger of cultural assimilation at the precise time that our wider culture is looking for new ideas and alternative answers. Thank God, then, for Mike's message, which calls us back to the glorious weirdness of the gospel.

PETE GREIG, team leader of 24-7 Prayer International, senior pastor of Emmaus Rd, and author of *Dirty Glory*

Michael Frost reminds us with winsome prose and challenging clarity that if our neighbors don't see us living out our Christian faith together as alternative story, something has gone horribly wrong. Read this book and ignore the noise of conformity. If we do, the best days of the local church are just ahead of us.

TIM SOERENS, cofounder of Parish Collective and coauthor of *The New Parish*

Following the apostle Paul's advice to the Roman church, "Do not conform to the pattern of this world," Michael Frost offers us a poignant meditation on the weirdness of our Christian faith. *Keep Christianity Weird* is the irresistible sort of book that I will read and reread to remind myself what it means to follow in the way of Jesus and in the footsteps of the faithful cloud of witnesses who have gone before us.

C. CHRISTOPHER SMITH, founding editor of *The Englewood Review of Books* and coauthor of the award-winning book *Slow Church*

Keep Christianity Weird is a provocative book, but only for people who need to be provoked. For the rest of us—people who need a fresh reminder of the Good News or the great commission—this book is a gift.

DAVE FERGUSON, lead pastor of Community Christian Church and author of *Hero Maker: Five Essential Practices for Leaders to Multiply Leaders*

Michael Frost calls us away from a generic, domesticated, deistic gospel and back into a wild, incarnate, neighborhood-focused, authentically weird, attractive Christianity—which looks, oddly enough, just like Jesus and his Kingdom come.

AUBREY SAMPSON, church planter, teaching pastor, and author of *Overcomer* and *The Louder Song* (2019)

This book does not disappoint. With Michael's usual mix of biblical and historical wisdom, cultural exegesis, and keen wit, Michael invites us to be God's peculiar people in the best possible ways.

DANIEL FUSCO, pastor of Crossroads Community Church and author of *Upward, Inward, Outward* and *Honestly*

Michael Frost invites us to open our eyes to the way of the Master and to reimagine what it means to be the people of God in our time. He looks at Jesus (the original weirdo) and numerous biblical and historical figures whose unusual ways of relating to the world around them reflected the Kingdom of God and brought about miraculous change. Michael reminds us of things we may have forgotten. Hold on tight.

AL ENGLER, director of Navigators Neighbors and Navigators Workplace

KEEP CHRIST-IANITY WEIRD.

GRACIOUS
LOVING
KIND
GENEROUS
GENTLE
PROVOCATIVE
PATIENT
SURPRISING
WINSOME

Embracing
the Discipline
of Being
Different

MICHAEL FROST

AUTHOR OF *SURPRISE THE WORLD*

NAVPRESS

A NavPress resource published in alliance
with Tyndale House Publishers, Inc.

NAVPRESS ⬤.

NavPress is the publishing ministry of The Navigators, an international Christian organization and leader in personal spiritual development. NavPress is committed to helping people grow spiritually and enjoy lives of meaning and hope through personal and group resources that are biblically rooted, culturally relevant, and highly practical.

For more information, visit www.NavPress.com.

Keep Christianity Weird: Embracing the Discipline of Being Different

Copyright © 2018 by Michael Frost. All rights reserved.

A NavPress resource published in alliance with Tyndale House Publishers, Inc.

NAVPRESS and the NAVPRESS logo are registered trademarks of NavPress, The Navigators, Colorado Springs, CO. *TYNDALE* is a registered trademark of Tyndale House Publishers, Inc. Absence of ® in connection with marks of NavPress or other parties does not indicate an absence of registration of those marks.

The Team: Don Pape, Publisher; David Zimmerman, Acquisitions Editor; Elizabeth Symm, Copy Editor; Jennifer Phelps, Designer

Cover title illustration by Jennifer Phelps. Copyright © Tyndale House Publishers, Inc. All rights reserved.

For information about special discounts for bulk purchases, please contact Tyndale House Publishers at csresponse@tyndale.com, or call 1-800-323-9400.

Cataloging-in-Publication Data is available.

ISBN 978-1-63146-851-3

Printed in Canada

24	23	22	21	20	19	18
7	6	5	4	3	2	1

FOR CAZ

CONTENTS

INTRODUCTION

In 2015, I published a little book entitled *Surprise the World: The Five Habits of Highly Missional People*. It was a short manual on how to foster the kind of alternative Christian lifestyle that would be likely to, well, *surprise* our neighbors and provoke them to ask us about our faith. I was really trying to help Christians develop the habits that would shape them into generous, hospitable, Spirit-led, Christlike missionaries. As I explained in that book, it was their very difference from their dominant culture that made the early church such an intriguing community in its first few centuries of existence. And that intrigue led people to explore the beliefs that cultivated such a winsome community.

Today, church attendance, while becoming ever less popular, isn't an intriguing act. Indeed, in some quarters, just saying you're a Christian might conjure the assumption that you're a fundamentalist right-wing homophobe. It's become more repellent than intriguing.

Surprise the World was my attempt to help Christians think about what alternative practices, beyond mere church attendance, would arouse the curiosity of others, and to show the overwhelming goodness of the Kingdom of God.

My fear, however, has been that too many churches might have used that book simply to promote the five habits as a short-term project bolted on to the many other programs the church conducts. Many pastors contacted me to say they were doing a *Surprise the World* month in their small-group ministries and preaching through the contents of the book. Don't get me wrong, I was delighted to see so many people taking that book to heart. But I'm afraid a month of promoting the five habits won't yield very much unless we can nurture a more pervasive worldview in our churches, one that sees the inherent weirdness, or strangeness, of the Christian experience. This was the key to my five missional habits: They must be *habits*. They must be expressions of a genuinely alternative lifestyle, one that shows our neighbors that there's a different—indeed better—way to be human in this world.

Stanley Hauerwas writes, "Nothing enslaves more than that which we think we cannot live without."[1] And here is an important point. If our churches are filled with people living the same way everybody else does, what do we have to commend? Information on how to go to heaven when you die? What about helping people become fully alive now! Our churches need to be full of people who have been truly set free from that which enslaves the world and who can show others how Jesus makes that possible. Learning fresh habits helps. But we also need to be freed from that which we cannot live without. Later in his commentary on Matthew's Gospel, Hauerwas, writing about the Lord's Prayer and the Sermon on the Mount, says,

> To be formed in the habits, the virtues, of the prayer we are taught to pray means that Christians cannot help but appear as a threat to the legitimating ideologies of those who rule. Christians do not seek to be subversives; it just turns out that living according to the Sermon on the Mount cannot help but challenge the way things are.[2]

The book you are now reading is my humble attempt to encourage you to challenge the way things are by living a life that has been truly set free by Christ. Consider it a kind of companion piece to *Surprise the World*, a little less practical, but absolutely essential in cultivating a highly missional people.

1

HERE'S TO THE CRAZY ONES

Blessed are the weird people . . .
Poets, misfits, writers, mystics, heretics,
Painters, and troubadours . . .
For they teach us to see the world through different eyes.

JACOB NORDBY

In 1997, Apple launched its now-iconic "Think Different" advertising campaign, featuring black-and-white footage of groundbreakers like Albert Einstein, Bob Dylan, Martin Luther King, John Lennon, Mahatma Gandhi, Pablo Picasso, and others, and voiced by actor Richard Dreyfuss, intoning, "Here's to the crazy ones."

To this day, there's debate about who actually wrote the copy for the "Think Different" commercial.[1] Most agree it was largely the work of Rob Siltanen, a creative director and a managing partner of the ad agency that produced it. But like all ad campaigns, it was a collaboration that included contributions by Steve Jobs himself and various members of the team from the agency. In any case, the "Think Different" voiceover is one of the truly great pieces of advertising copy ever written:

> Here's to the crazy ones. The misfits. The rebels. The troublemakers. The round pegs in the square holes. The ones who see things differently. They're not fond of rules. And they have no respect for the status quo. You can quote them, disagree with them, glorify or vilify them. About the only thing you can't do is ignore them. Because they change things. They push the human race forward. And while some may see them as the crazy ones, we see genius. Because the people who are crazy enough to think they can change the world, are the ones who do.[2]

You can hear a hint of Robert Frost and Jack Kerouac and even a touch of Kurt Vonnegut in the cadence of the language. But that's not the only reason why it's so good. It works because it resonates so strongly with us all. Everyone who appears in the "Think Different" campaign really did epitomize the spirit of the campaign. They broke the rules, they were vilified, but they changed stuff. Dylan, Lennon, Gandhi, Ali, and King all drove their contemporaries around the bend. But looking back, we now view them as groundbreakers who left the world a better place. We all know it's true that crazy people change the world.

So here's my question: Why isn't there a bit more crazy in Christianity these days? And I don't mean crazy as in zany or juvenile (there's plenty of *that*!). I mean crazy as in Picasso, Jim Henson, Martha Graham, and Cesar Chavez. I mean crazy as in round pegs in square holes. Could it be that the church has closed its doors to the misfits and rebels and troublemakers? Does the church make space for and foster the contributions of those who see things differently? If Steve Jobs was right and the world is pushed forward by people who break the rules and have no respect for the status quo, what does that say about the church's vision to change the world?

ECCENTRIC CHRISTIANS

Not that it's always been this way. In fact, the church has produced these "crazy ones" in the past (MLK being a case in point), and while their contemporaries might have viewed them askance, they are widely regarded as those who pushed the cause of Christ forward.

St. Boniface was an eighth-century Scottish missionary to Germany who became frustrated with the Germanic pagans' devotion to a sacred oak tree worshiped to honor Thor. The Germans feared that to even touch the tree would bring down the wrath of the gods. So Boniface took an axe to the oak, and having felled it, used the wood to build a church at the site dedicated to St. Peter. That's pretty crazy.

Francis Xavier, one of the craziest evangelists in history, having established Christianity in western India and the East Indies, met a samurai warrior named Anjirō in Malacca in 1547. Anjirō was on the run from the Japanese authorities, having killed a man there. Francis shared the message of Christ's forgiveness with Anjirō, who accepted Christianity and decided to return to Japan to face the music. But he also begged Francis to accompany him and to bring the gospel to his homeland. Remember, this was 1547! Francis had already traveled from his native Portugal to India to modern-day Indonesia. Asking him to go to Japan may well have been like inviting us to the moon. But he agreed, and became the first Christian missionary to the closed kingdom.

Or there's the exotically named Count Nikolaus von Zinzendorf, who virtually relinquished his highborn status to join a band of traveling asylum seekers from Moravia and Bohemia (the Czech Republic today) who had camped on his estate in Germany in 1722. The Moravians were a disorderly bunch, but nonetheless, the temporary village they created on Zinzendorf's estate soon became a refuge of religious freedom that attracted persecuted Christians from across Europe. But these people were persecuted because of their passionately held views, so as Zinzendorf's model village swelled with fanatics from differing perspectives, things got very rowdy. Differing factions charged each other with heresy, and their leaders accused each other of being false prophets. Things heated up when these leaders started trading apocalyptic visions at a hundred paces. The village fell into disarray and serious conflict.

Most of Europe's landed gentry, when faced with a disorderly mob camped out on their estate, would have simply and quickly evicted them and been done with it. But not Zinzendorf. He joined them!

He pretty much left his castle to live in the Moravian village, to pray and minister to each family, and to call on them to live together in love. That's just plain weird. But weirder still is the fact that God chose to use this strange community of refugees to ignite the modern missions movement. On August 13, 1727, the Holy Spirit descended on the village, bestowing what Zinzendorf later called "a sense of the nearness of Christ."[3] All their differences were blown away and this unlikely community became an extraordinary global missionary force.

I could go on. I could mention Anne Hutchinson from the Massachusetts Bay Colony, who was described as "a woman of a haughty and fierce carriage, of a nimble wit and active spirit, and a very voluble tongue, more bold than a man,"[4] whose crime—according to America's founding fathers—was usurping male authority. She was banished from the colony for her eccentricity.

Or Mother Ann Lee, the founder of the Shaker movement, whose views on equality between the sexes and her then-bizarre practice of speaking in multiple heavenly languages and worshiping by ecstatic dancing or "shaking" (hence the name) led to her being beaten regularly by mobs in England, and later, Massachusetts.

Or the fiery John Brown stirring up ferment against slavery in Kansas.

Or the hermit architect and devout Christian Antoni Gaudí designing the most curious buildings in Europe.

Or Albert Schweitzer madly playing Bach and Mendelssohn on his pedal piano in the Congolese jungle.

Or Stanley Jones hanging out with Mahatma Gandhi in his purpose-built Christian ashram in India.

Or Aimee Semple McPherson hamming it up in her extravagant set pieces every Sunday at Angelus Temple in Los Angeles (and even getting "kidnapped" to Mexico, but that's another story).

Or Arthur Blessitt, who started carrying a huge wooden cross around America in the 1960s and who has gone on to drag it faithfully all over the world (including over 300 countries and Antarctica).

They were the crazy ones. Round pegs in square holes.

And it feels as if there are fewer and fewer of them these days.

But before we imagine Christian eccentricity is the domain of just a few outstanding personalities, allow me to try to make a case for why *all* Christians should be eccentric.

The word eccentric comes from a combination of the Greek terms *ex* (out of) and *kentron* (center). When combined, *ekkentros* means "out of center." The term gained currency in the late Middle Ages, when astronomers like Copernicus dared to suggest that the earth was not at the center of the solar system. By claiming the earth in fact orbited the sun, Copernicus became the original eccentric.

Enter Richard Beck, a professor from Abilene Christian University, who pushes the definition of eccentricity a bit further. In his book *The Slavery of Death*, Beck takes its literal meaning ("out of center") and suggests that an eccentric identity is an identity where the focal point of the self is shifted to God. He says, "The ego, in a kind of Copernican Revolution, is displaced from the center and moved to the periphery. The self is displaced being the 'center of the universe' so that it may orbit God."[5]

In other words, all Christians who have made God the center and focus of their lives can rightly be called eccentric.

The alternative, Beck says, is what Martin Luther called *incurvatus in se*, the self "curved inward" upon itself, with the ego at the center of our identity. "*Incurvatus in se* suggests that human sinfulness is rooted in self-focus, self-absorption, and self-worship."[6] It's me at the center. A true conversion to Christ involves displacing me and becoming truly "off center."

Now, of course, that's not how we usually use the term *eccentric*. When we think of people who are "off center," the center we have in mind is usually some cultural or behavioral norm. So eccentric people are those who act in a socially unorthodox fashion. They're strange, unusual, sometimes deviant. But Beck is trying to rehabilitate the term, to drive us back to its original meaning and to suggest eccentricity should not only be expressed in zany behavior but also in truly biblical Christianity. When we put God at the center of our identity and push our egos out to the edge, we will become a different kind of people. He says,

Eccentric Christianity is a new orbit where the self is displaced and God is found at the center of life. And in this displacement the Christian begins to act in "strange and unusual ways" in relation to the norms of the world.

We become, in the words of the King James Version, "a peculiar people."[7]

In my previous book *Surprise the World*, I make the case that the early church eventually usurped and conquered the Roman world by living such a sublimely alternative lifestyle that they attracted thousands of people bowed and broken by the cruelty of life under Caesar. These Christians were a peculiar people. Or, as I pointed out in that book, they lived "questionable lives."[8]

Today, the church in America seems to have traded in its mandate to be eccentric and aimed instead at an unconscious conventionality. Rural norms are too quaint, urban norms too dangerous, so the church finds a happy medium in a suburban spirituality. It's impolite to think of ourselves as rich and demoralizing to think of ourselves as poor, so we find a happy medium in the middle class. We are happy. We are medium. We fit in. And very often we baptize that conventionality by suggesting that God is primarily concerned with order, and with us living peaceably with our neighbors. I'm certainly not suggesting we shouldn't be peaceable, but neither should we be indistinguishable from our fine, upstanding non-Christian neighbors.

We're the "off center" ones. Or, at least, we should be.

THE ECCENTRIC GOD

If Richard Beck's more psychological argument about displacing the ego and orbiting our identity around

God isn't convincing enough (he is a professor of psychology, after all), he also offers a handy theological basis for eccentricity as well: *God is eccentric.*

Yep, we have an eccentric God. Think about it. While many religions see their deities being intrinsically bound up in creation, the biblical God is "off center." The God of the Bible is separate from the created world. Certainly, God is involved in the created world. God draws close to his people. He's described as sustaining the universe and involving himself in human affairs. And he is revealed to us most clearly as the enfleshed Messiah, Jesus. All that is true.

But orthodox Christianity teaches that the triune God remains wholly Other, separate from the universe he has created. Beck puts it this way:

> The eccentric God is always experienced as
> "outside" the system and status quo. God
> approaches us from "the outside" of our current
> arrangements and understandings. Consequently,
> when it comes to God the community of faith
> has to adopt a *receptive posture*, waiting upon
> the initiative of God. And while all this is often
> described with the language of "transcendence"—
> using a higher vs. lower metaphor—it can also
> be described by the eccentric metaphor, an inside
> vs. outside distinction.[9]

He's right. God is holy, ineffable (indescribable), beyond. And there's something thoroughly eccentric about that. It means God can never be captured or made "ours." If God exists beyond us, God can't be circumscribed or reduced to our agendas or systems. I'm not suggesting we can't know God. In Christ, God has reached out to us. God desires relationship with us and has shown us great mercy and kindness. But we don't get to own God.

God is not an American or Australian. God is not middle class. God is not black. Or white. Or poor. Or rich. Or Southern Baptist. Or Pentecostal. Or Republican. Or Democrat. Or any of the other containers we try to put him in. He's an eccentric God, and an eccentric God is free—truly, utterly free.

And we need this truly, utterly free God, because all of us (conservatives and liberals, left and right) are so profoundly tempted to align the voice of God with our own voice.

As Richard Beck points out, to be a genuinely eccentric people, we need to serve an eccentric God, one that "cannot be bounded, encircled or delimited to our group, our interests, our values, our nation, our way of life, our choices, our worldview, our economy, our church, or our theology."[10]

In other words, if we can make God captive to our cultural preferences, then we will most certainly ourselves be captive to them too. We have to learn the often-challenging truth that God exists beyond our agendas, which in turn could free us from our own unhelpful, even ungodly, plans and schemes.

But there's more. Beck adds a third dimension to this discussion of eccentricity—the Kingdom of God is eccentric.

We know the Kingdom of God isn't a specific territory. The Kingdom of God is like salt and light. Like God, it cannot be contained or walled in to a particular zone. It's not like America is Kingdom-of-God territory and Syria isn't. The very character of God's Kingdom is alternate to the character and values of this world. It doesn't create borders and defend them. It doesn't foster parochialism or insist on pledges of allegiances to particular flags. Its values are justice, reconciliation, beauty, and wholeness. It can't easily be identified in conventional, observable ways. Jesus said as much when the Pharisees challenged him to show them this kingdom he was speaking about. He replied, "The coming of the kingdom of God is not something that can be observed, nor will people say, 'Here it is,' or 'There it is,' because the kingdom of God is in your midst" (Luke 17:20-21). Similarly, Richard Beck says,

> The eccentric Kingdom doesn't claim territory over against the world. The eccentric Kingdom

doesn't erect walls to create a gated community. . . . The eccentric Kingdom is the embedded, pilgrim, landless, possessionless, homeless, sojourning, itinerant missionary community called and commissioned to live lives of radical service and availability to the world.[11]

Wow.

ROUND PEGS IN SQUARE HOLES OR SQUARE PEGS IN ROUND HOLES?

Apple's "Think Different" ad quirkily referred to round pegs in square holes, even though the common expression is "a square peg in a round hole." It seems the campaign writers were willing to be eccentric even in their use of idioms. The challenge of eccentric Christianity is that quirks so regularly get mainstreamed into the dominant culture: Round pegs are hammered uncomfortably into square holes, or even—sometimes—offered round holes in exchange for their compliance. What began as surprising over time becomes unremarkable. So the call to be eccentric people serving an eccentric God, and sent out to alert others to the eccentric Kingdom, involves a call to perseverance, an active resistance to domestication.

I think we should all be striving to dethrone our egos

and have our identities shaped by God as our center. We should all be seeking to become more off-center. But in our general attempts to become the eccentric Christians we're meant to be, it appears that God gives us certain "crazy ones" who seem freer to embody the faith. They are beacons to us. Indications of the life we were set free from in order to live. The John Browns or Aimee Semple McPhersons seem more capable of throwing off convention than the rest of us. We need to find these people and value them.

Of course, the church has a habit of either banishing or killing their crazies. But they are essential to the church's health and future. In a fascinating study in *Scientific American*, Shelley Carson examined why creative people are more eccentric than the rest of us. She concludes that it partly has to do with brain function. Studies have shown that highly creative individuals are more likely to display something called cognitive disinhibition. That's the tendency to indulge in information that is irrelevant to whatever you're working on or thinking about. Most of us inhibit or filter irrelevant information when we're concentrating on a particular task. But creative people don't do that. They let it all come flooding in.

Carson sees this cognitive disinhibition as "likely at the heart of what we think of as the *aha!* experience. During moments of insight, cognitive filters relax momentarily and allow ideas that are on the brain's back burners to leap forward into conscious awareness."[12] Kind of like Russell Crowe's depiction of John Nash in *A Beautiful Mind*, or Benedict Cumberbatch's portrayal of Alan Turing in *The Imitation Game*. Their breakthrough ideas seem to catch even them by surprise.

Responding to all this stimulus can make creative types seem less interested in the mundane or the everyday. They're not so concerned about the state of their dress. Or with learning the strictures of polite conversation. So they seem eccentric or outlandish. In her own research into eccentricity, Shelly Carson asks subjects, "Do you often feel like a square peg in a round hole?" (That phrase again!) Participants who score high on the creativity scale answer "yes" way more often than less creative participants. "In fact," Carson reports, "one participant—a Hollywood screenwriter—answered 'no' but then wrote below the question: 'I don't feel like a square peg trying to fit into a round hole. I feel like an octagonal peg with conical appendages.'"[13]

There's plenty of funding for studies in creativity and eccentricity, it turns out, because these kinds of people are good for business. They are highly prized in the marketplace. Carson reports that big corporations like Coca-Cola, DuPont, Citigroup, and Humana have recently created the position of CIO—chief innovation officer—as part of their leadership structure.

Accordingly, business schools like Harvard, Stanford, Columbia, and Yale now offer courses on creativity as part of their curricula. And Fortune 500 companies—including PepsiCo, Bristol-Myers Squibb, Aetna, and Marriott—are putting employees through creativity training programs to help non-eccentrics open their minds to out-of-the-box thoughts and stimuli that might otherwise be ignored or suppressed. Creativity is a highly sought-after commodity in the global market.

Celebrating this trend, and affirming those creatives who have not been silenced by convention, Shelley Carson concludes,

> Indeed, we all owe a deep debt of gratitude
> to those whose creative work has been
> accomplished at the expense of square-peg
> feelings of alienation and ostracism. The
> creative efforts of eccentrics add richness,
> beauty and innovation to the lives of
> those of us who have fit somewhat more
> comfortably into our round holes.[14]

So the broader culture increasingly recognizes the contribution of eccentricity to the greater good. But not the church. Just as business and education is fostering greater creativity and innovation, the church is in a phase of rewarding compliance and conservatism and suppressing eccentricity.

I'm not happy to do that. Are you? As Carson said, eccentrics add richness, beauty, and innovation to our lives. And Christian eccentrics can help push us forward into the things God has in store for us.

PAPA CHUCK AND THE JESUS FREAKS

But what if you're not a natural eccentric? What if you don't have cognitive disinhibition? What if you like coloring between the lines and you feel more like a round peg in a round hole? No worries. Lots of people—most people—are like that.

When it comes to cognitive disinhibition, I'm inclined to think that while some are naturally gifted, others need to develop it as a discipline. If we're going to embrace our calling as eccentric followers of an eccentric God, we need to be aware of those in our midst who are naturally inclined that way and be welcoming and supportive of them. But those of us who were not given the gift of cognitive disinhibition need to work at it. I'll explain how to do this later in this book, but for now, we need to understand that eccentricity might be a gift for some, or work for others, but we should all be looking for ways to increase our capacity for eccentricity as part of the normal Christian life.

From what Shelley Carson concludes, you don't have to be weird; you just need to foster environments where weird people are welcome and their contributions are encouraged, and where we can learn to be weirder from them. And my fear is that the church is not that kind of place. But as I've mentioned earlier, it hasn't always been that way. There have always been eccentric Christians, but it seems to me there's always also been a movement to suppress or domesticate them. We need to embrace the task of encouraging weirdos and unleashing them on the church. So if you're not crazy yourself, look to make space for some crazy.

A perfect, (relatively) recent example of this is the emergence of the Jesus People movement and the rise of its epicenter, Calvary Chapel in Costa Mesa, California.

Back in 1967, most churches across America were still singing hymns to pipe organs and robing their thirty-person choirs. Sermons were preached with a rhythmic authoritative cadence unlike ordinary speech. And ministers were as revered as bank managers and school principals. They combed Brylcreem through their hair and wore blazers and ties as streetwear.

But 1967 was also the Summer of Love in San Francisco, and thousands of young people were descending on the Haight-Ashbury district and filtering down into Southern California, attracted by promises of free love, psychedelic drugs, and great surf. They were rejecting the materialist world and middle-class ideals of their parents and their Brylcreemed ministers. They embraced the hippie lifestyle—anticonsumerist, off-the-grid, and definitely alternative.

But not all eccentricity is healthy (more on that later), and for many of these young people, the promises made in the songs of the Mamas and the Papas and the Grateful Dead were never fulfilled. The dark side of the Summer of Love was pretty dark indeed. Many ended up homeless and hungry in Southern California, easy prey to overdose, disease, and even cult leaders. And right in the middle of all this cultural upheaval was a conservative nondenominational preacher named Chuck Smith.

Chuck Smith was pretty much a minister right out of central casting. He didn't use Brylcreem because he was bald, but other than that, he'd fit right in at any traditional church across the country. He wore suits and ties and turtleneck sweaters and loved preaching forty-minute sermons. He held to all the mainstream values the hippie generation was rebelling against. But what marks "Papa Chuck" (as he became known) out from other ministers was that he loved crazies.

Chuck had founded Calvary Chapel in 1965 and soon discovered the streets and beaches around the church were littered with the flotsam rejected by the Haight-Ashbury culture. He and his wife, Kay, started taking drug-addled young vagrants into their home. Then he rented a house in Costa Mesa to serve as a Christian communal home and invited the kids to attend Calvary Chapel's Wednesday night Bible classes. Soon, thousands of "freaks" were attending these meetings.

Influenced more by the Beatles and the Beach Boys than by Isaac Watts and Charles Wesley, these new congregants began composing Christian folk songs, singing them in a huge circus tent Chuck had erected on church property. Thousands more began attending, and soon Papa Chuck was conducting mass baptisms below the ocean cliffs of Corona del Mar. No one knew it yet, but there amid a haze of drugs, folk music, and intense discussions about peace, love, and the gospel, the "Jesus freak" movement was about to be born.

The key to the success of Calvary Chapel, and the Jesus People movement it spawned, was Papa Chuck's acceptance of all comers. There was no dress code. The freaks could come as they were. He welcomed hippies, yippies, student activists, dropouts, and the drug-damaged. Inadvertently, Papa Chuck and the Jesus freaks were changing American Christianity as we know it. They invented a whole new style of worship, and from them emerged the charismatic movement, the contemporary Christian music scene, even the church growth and "seeker-sensitive" movements.

Whether you love everything about the kind of church that arose in the 1980s and beyond and whether you agree with everything Chuck Smith said or stood for is beside the point. The point is that Calvary Chapel was cognitively disinhibited enough to see a place for a generation of young people who otherwise would not have darkened the door of a church.

Part of Papa Chuck's genius was that he was theologically conservative but simultaneously culturally avant-garde. He knew the importance of making space for eccentricity and creativity. I suspect that God was on the move in the 1960s and 1970s, loosening up the American church, pushing them into the kind of eccentricity Richard Beck talks about. And while Chuck Smith wasn't the naturally eccentric kind of leader who could have taken the church there, he was comfortable enough with freaks to allow them to make a contribution.

I can think of several examples of how more socially conventional leaders opened the church to the voices of a more eccentric form of Christianity. In 1974, the Anglican rector John Stott used his position as a universally respected evangelical leader to intentionally incorporate the contributions of the Latin American leaders of the integral mission movement at the International Congress on World Evangelization in Lausanne. The congress had been established by

Billy Graham with the theme "Let the Earth Hear His Voice," and might have just stuck with discussing the whats, whys, and hows of successful evangelization had it not been for the emergence of firebrand student leaders from Peru like René Padilla, Pedro Arana, and Samuel Escobar.

Padilla, Arana, and Escobar went to Lausanne to ensure that social justice was not marginalized from the discussion. They referred to their approach of integrating evangelism and social action as "integral mission," and in the strife-torn and poverty-stricken nations of Latin and South America, they considered it essential to successful mission. Suspecting that the Lausanne delegates might champion evangelism to the exclusion of justice ministries in reaction to a number of previous missionary conferences that had done the reverse, Padilla, Arana, and Escobar invited Stott to see what integral mission looked like in Peru.

Looking at old photos from Stott's visit to Peru, you see the cultural and generational differences quite starkly. Stott was a square—a kindly Anglican minister, dressed conservatively and smiling politely for the camera. The Peruvians, meanwhile, wore natty safari suits and floral shirts and sported pencil mustaches and long hair. Nevertheless, Stott was impressed with what he saw and heard. And when they all got to Lausanne, Stott held the door open for them.

The result was the highly influential Lausanne Covenant. It affirms social justice, values the integration of word and deed, and declares the importance of evangelism. And the evangelical world hasn't been the same since.

Maybe an even more contemporary example than Chuck Smith or John Stott is that of Jorge Mario Bergoglio. Untroubled by fear of controversy, and genuinely compassionate toward the outsider, Pope Francis (as he is now known) is stirring up the Catholic church, creating an environment where fresh voices and new perspectives can at last be heard. Who knows where it will lead, but Francis has demonstrated his own eccentricity, and his church is finally safe for eccentrics to play in. The first pope from the Franciscan order, he is a living reminder of his namesake, Francis of Assisi. There has hardly been a more eccentric Christian than he was.

What about you? What scares you about the crazy ones? Whose voices are you least likely to listen to? How might you imagine they would change your life for the better? And what about your church? Whose voices are unheard? Is it a safe, generative space for the crazy ones, the misfits, the rebels, the troublemakers, the round pegs in the square holes? Because if it's not, the church is the poorer.

FOR YOUR CONSIDERATION

1. Who are some historical (or contemporary) people you particularly admire? Why? What, if anything, is eccentric about those people?

2. When you think about the "eccentricity" of Christianity, what comes to mind first? Why?

3. What fears do you have about allowing eccentric Christians to make a greater contribution to your church?

4. Where do you fall on a spectrum of conventional to crazy? How do you feel you fit in to this vision of the Christian faith? Why?

2

WHAT ARE WEIRD CITIES TELLING US?

Suburban values: cleanliness, orderliness, safety—
dullness, in other words.

REM KOOLHAAS

Fostering a Christian form of eccentricity is essential, as we've seen. It's the direct result of dethroning ourselves as the center of our own universes, and it provides forums for creative eccentrics to innovate and push the church forward.

But there's another reason for embracing off-centeredness. The world is yearning for it. In mirroring the cultural blandness of contemporary life, many churches are signing their own death warrants, because the kids and now the grandkids of baby boomers desire something more diverse, more interesting, more culturally rich than the mildness that dominates the cultural landscape. Eccentric Christianity needs to lead the way in shaping the future rather than wedding itself to the increasingly outmoded forms of culture. The church should be teaching the world to be weird in the way of Jesus.

In calling this book *Keep Christianity Weird*, I'm riffing off the slogan used by a number of American cities that are intentionally trying to combat the worst impulses of suburban culture. Cities like Portland and Austin are holding out against consumerism and over-development and championing environmentalism and social justice. Their example can help us recover the church's eccentric capacity to defy the worst aspects of what's disparagingly called "Generica."

VISIONS OF GENERICA

Maybe you remember Tim Burton's 1990 film *Edward Scissorhands* and its devastating depiction of American suburban culture. Burton dreamed up the story of the freakish kid with scissors for hands trying to fit in to bland suburbia when he was just a teenager struggling with his own sense of isolation and his inability to communicate with people around him as a kid.

Burton grew up in Burbank, California, a suburban community in the greater Los Angeles area. By the time he was thirty-two and finally filming the story, Burbank had changed too much to be used as the set for the movie, so production moved to Tampa Bay, Florida, where production designer Bo Welch found "a kind of generic, plain-wrap suburb, which we made even more characterless by painting all the houses in faded pastels, and reducing the window sizes to make it look a little more paranoid."[1]

If you watch the film now, it's hard to believe it was actually a real neighborhood and not a fake movie set. The identical double-fronted houses are each painted a different color—pastel green, pink, yellow, and blue. Or as Welch called them, "sea-foam green, dirty flesh, butter, and dirty blue."[2] Each house has a pastel-colored car in the driveway, but not one that matches the house. A pink house will have a green car, and a blue house a yellow car, and so forth. The suburban housewives in the film also wear pastels in four shades. And of course, all the houses are enveloped in perfectly manicured lawns and neatly trimmed sidewalks.

It was all designed to depict suburban life as relentlessly bland, featureless, and uniform.

This was suburbia in the 1960s and 1970s, and the apotheosis of its blandness during this era was undoubtedly the ubiquitous American strip mall. Strip malls really are the ultimate expression of post-war suburbia—nondescript, beige, single-story, automobile-friendly shopping centers built along the main roads, a line of shops standing shoulder to shoulder, bravely facing their sprawling parking lots. There's really nothing like them anywhere else in the world. And for good reason. Only the most car-addicted nation in the world could invent the strip mall.

This is the world Tim Burton grew up in, but by the time he was depicting that world in *Edward Scissorhands*, suburban planning was changing. In the 1990s, the principles of what became known as New Urbanism were becoming popular. Recognizing the ways post-war Modernism had destroyed neighborhoods, the New Urbanists tried to create a different kind of suburb, a more community-minded neighborhood. Designer Chris DeWolf defines New Urbanism this way:

> Since the early 1990s New Urbanism has slowly gathered strength, a building storm that finally burst onto the American mainstream only a few years ago. Its "neotraditional" principles—wide sidewalks and narrow streets, front porches and rear garages, central squares and shopping districts—garnered attention across Canada and the United States. Some of the communities that resulted tried to emulate small towns while others resembled urban neighbourhoods. In the end, however, their goal was the same: create new developments that are community- and people-oriented.[3]

To see what they had in mind, we can turn to another film, Peter Weir's *The Truman Show*. Made in 1998, *The Truman Show* stars Jim Carrey as a man raised from childhood by a corporation inside a huge Hollywood soundstage, designed to be the fictitious seaside village of Seahaven. Weir envisioned Seahaven to be an entirely artificial community, a brand-new version of a Norman Rockwell painting. Seahaven was to be quainter than quaint. Initially, Weir thought he would need to create the sets on a soundstage, until he was told about the real-life suburb of Seaside, a master-planned estate in Florida. Seaside was one of the first built-to-order New Urbanist communities—it stood in for the banality and fake nostalgic imagery of Seahaven perfectly.

Carrey's character, Truman Burbank, seems happy enough in the perfectly perfect town of Seahaven, but the underlying premise of the film is that he's trapped in his gilded cage. We the audience find ourselves willing him to escape, to fly to Fiji (his ultimate dream), or to sail his small boat to freedom, to discover the world beyond the dome.

It was somewhat brazen of Peter Weir to make a film that parodies New Urbanism in its darling project of Seaside. People-oriented housing developments can't be bad, can they? But if you've ever visited a New Urbanist development, you'll know there's something pretty Trumanesque about them. They're faux towns trying to resemble prewar small towns, full of brick townhouses, white picket fences, and Colonial homes. You can eat at a pizza restaurant that looks like a renovated and repurposed old fire station, except you know it was built that way to begin with. There's a man-made lake in the middle of town that looks and feels, well, man-made. In other words, New Urbanism creates a contrived atmosphere. DeWolf concludes, "Instead of actually being successful urban neighbourhoods, New Urbanist developments simply *look like* urban neighbourhoods" (emphasis added).[4]

If the worst of Tim Burton's suburban nightmare is the strip mall, the worst expression of New Urbanism is the faux town square. Sometimes styled a "suburban lifestyle center," these town squares usually come replete with a fountain, outdoor dining for franchised restaurants, and Euro-style townhouses. Hey, it looks much better than a strip mall, but it seems to create no more community. Faux town squares are usually empty, especially during the day.

In fact, architect Michael Sorkin called New Urbanism "the acceptable face of sprawl," and wrote that it "reproduces many of the worst aspects of the modernism it seeks to replace. . . . [It] promotes another style of universality that . . . is similarly overreliant on visual cues in attempting to produce social effects."[5]

In other words, whether it's the old Tim Burton

version or the new Seahaven version, suburbia hasn't changed much in half a century.

I find it interesting that while we watch films like these—and we could add *Pleasantville*, *Buffy the Vampire Slayer*, and television shows like *Desperate Housewives* and many more to the list—and find ourselves laughing condescendingly at vapid suburban life, the fact is that most Americans grow up in suburbs. Forty-four million Americans live in the nation's 51 major metropolitan areas, while nearly 122 million live in their suburbs. In other words, nearly three quarters of metropolitan Americans live in suburbs, not urban centers. And not just the predominantly white suburbs of *Edward Scissorhands* or *The Truman Show*. According to the *Washington Post*, "One-third of suburbanites across the country are racial or ethnic minorities, up from 19 percent in 1990. Students in suburban public schools are 20 percent Hispanic, 15 percent African American, and 6 percent Asian American."[6] For better or worse, the suburbs are a reflection of America.

In fact, suburbia has been so popular that, according to the American Farmland Trust, the United States loses more than forty acres of farmland every hour to new development. Between 1982 and 2010, new development devoured the equivalent acreage of Indiana and Rhode Island combined.[7]

Because of the rapid growth and cultural normal-ization of the suburban experience, the suburbs became the overwhelmingly dominant mission field of new churches. Most of the churches across America were planted and grown in the soil of postwar suburbia. The whole idea of the American suburb was created by two complementary forces. One was the desperate need to provide housing for the millions of servicemen return-ing from the war. The other was the development of the interstate highway system. These two things made Americans more mobile and housing more available. People could now work in one part of a city and live in another. There's much that could be said about how housing developers and car manufacturers have totally altered the American landscape—physically, environ-mentally, socially, politically, sexually, and racially. But allow me to say that the popular depictions of suburbia we've looked at present it pretty much as a place of con-formity, complacency, conservatism, and boredom.

But things are changing. Like Truman, there are thousands of people who grew up in suburbs and want to get out. Like Truman, they want to be explorers. They want to visit Fiji—or their version of Fiji, which may not be an island in the middle of the Pacific. It could be just across the country in one of the increasing number of cities that are eschewing the master-planned nature of Generica.

A number of cities across the US are figuring out that more and more people who grew up in Pleasantville want something, well, weirder.

PROMOTING WEIRDNESS

In 2000, Austin, Texas, adopted as its slogan "Keep Austin Weird." Generated as a grassroots movement, "Keep Austin Weird" became a rallying cry for local business, a sense of neighborhood, and a zone for creative resistance.[8] The slogan, or variations of it (like "Keep Knoxville Shabby"), have since been appropriated by Santa Cruz, Portland, and a bunch of other cities across the US.

Initially just a promotional tagline, "Keep [enter city name] Weird" was more seriously interrogated by Joshua Long in his 2010 book, *Weird City*. He defined the Weird City doctrine as a combination of attachment to a sense of place, more socially and environmentally responsible consumption patterns, sustainable development, and urban politics. The Weird City doctrine values such things as the beautification of the built environment, resistance to gentrification, the promotion of boutique local industries, being a refuge for alternative lifestyles, addressing homelessness in more meaningful ways, and generally defying the cultural trends that make many other American cities virtually interchangeable.

Of course, the most obvious question to ask is: What are they keeping Austin weird *from*? What was trying to unweird the city? In his book, Long lists a set of weird values the residents of Austin were eager to hold on to:

- Keep Austin music noncorporate, creative, and independent.
- Keep Austin laid-back, antimaterialistic, and not worried about the rat race of everyday life.
- Keep Austin nonconformist, unique, tolerant, and supportive of cultural and artistic expression.
- Keep Austin neighborhoods unique, community oriented, and connected.
- Keep Austin from overdeveloping and becoming homogenized.
- Keep Austin environmentally friendly and aware.
- Keep Austin different and opposed to conservative, red-state, bucolic Texas.
- Keep Austin locally owned, independent, and community-oriented.
- Keep Austin unique, with iconic and quirky landmarks, buildings, traditions, and festivals.[9]

From this list you can see that for the Weird Cities movement, the enemies of weirdness are materialism, conformity, homogeneity, environmental unsustainability, political conservatism, and corporate America (particularly housing developers). In other words, it can be seen as a direct reaction to the values of suburbia.

Of course, over the years, the Weird City reputation has been lampooned as a blend of drum circles, kooky politics, surfing Santas, and the guy in Portland who rides a unicycle while playing a flaming bagpipe. But at its best, Weird City thinking is a resistance to the Generica of big-box stores, identical strip malls, and color-coordinated housing developments. It is similar to social movements like the slow-food movement, the farm-to-table movement, and other antiglobalization and anticonsumerism initiatives. And young people are streaming to weird cities like Austin, Portland, and Santa Cruz, as well as towns embracing their emerging weirdness like Asheville, North Carolina; Boulder, Colorado; and Ithaca, New York. Similar cities like Forth Worth, Kansas City, and Denver are also seeing a renaissance.

The kids who grew up in planned suburbs, shopping at strip malls or hanging out at fake town squares want to live in places that are *real*. They want community-oriented neighborhoods. They want diverse, connected, creative, energizing places to live. They want to shop in local stores, owned and managed by locals, selling locally (or close to locally) produced goods. They want environmentally friendly neighborhoods that connect them to the geography around them.

I suspect they don't want weirdness in the Austin sense of the term, but they want their city to be, well, *weird*.

And they're voting with their feet. Or their wallets.

The movement of young adults out of the suburbs is now contributing to what economists and urban planners are calling the early stages of the death of suburbia. And the symptoms of its demise are pretty obvious. They include the following economic indicators:

No one wants a McMansion anymore

In August 2016, *Bloomberg* quoted the real-estate site Trulia saying that sales of huge (between 3,000 and 5,000 square feet), cheaply constructed, off-the-plan mansions have dropped dramatically in 85 of the country's 100 biggest cities. In one cited example, in Fort Lauderdale, the extra money that buyers were expected to be willing to pay to own a McMansion fell by 84 percent from 2012 to 2016.[10] A *Business Insider* article recently stated that "the youngest generations of homebuyers tend to value efficiency more than ever before and feel that McMansions are impractical and wasteful."[11] Also, with family sizes becoming much smaller, the idea of living in a cavernous mansion has been dismissed as ridiculous.

Malls have become ghost towns

Maybe you've visited a suburban mall recently and wondered where all the people are. Or where all the stores are. Empty shop-fronts aren't just bad for mall ambience; they signal a shift in where younger people like to shop. And it's not just the closure of small retailers that mall owners have to worry about. Department stores like Macy's, Sears, and JCPenney are referred to in commercial speak as "anchor stores." It's always been believed if a mall has a couple of anchor stores it can't fail. But all three of those aforementioned department stores are currently closing hundreds of locations. CoStar, a real estate firm, predicts that "nearly a quarter of malls in the US, or roughly 310 of the nation's 1,300 shopping malls, are at high risk of losing an anchor store."[12]

Millennials have discovered their kitchens

While boomers loved eating out and remained intensely loyal to their favorite casual dining chains, millennials want to prepare healthier food at home.

As a result, the casual-dining industry is in freefall. In 2017, Ruby Tuesday sold ninety-five restaurants. Outback Steakhouse and Carrabba's Italian Grill are in big trouble. Buffalo Wild Wings is seeing sales plummet. And if shopping malls keep failing, we can say goodbye to food-court mainstays like Sbarro, Cinnabon, Jamba Juice, and Panda Express.

All the while, most of my favorite podcasts are being sponsored by businesses like Blue Apron. Maybe you've heard your favorite podcasters reading their commercials about how they'll design your menu and send you "perfectly portioned ingredients and step-by-step recipes" so you can "cook healthy food, sustainably sourced, and at a better price." Blue Apron might be the best-known meal delivery service, but right behind them are recent start-ups like Plated, Hello Fresh, and a bunch of others, who know that millennials don't want to eat regularly at The Cheesecake Factory or Red Lobster.

In saying this, I'm not suggesting that these meal delivery services are the way of the future. Neither am I saying they are necessarily ethically superior to chain restaurants. And every time I hear an announcer promoting one of these services by salivating about braised butternut squash pasta with miso kale, farro, persimmon, and goat cheese salad, I can't help thinking how elitist it all sounds. It's essentially a perpetual catering service for young professionals. But it does signal their desire to get cooking.

Some years ago, I stayed in the home of a couple of baby-boomer empty nesters. Their kitchen pantry was almost completely empty. When I jokingly commented on this to the male partner, he laughed and told me they ate out all the time. Then he opened the pristinely clean oven to reveal a beautifully wrapped gift box. He told me he was hiding his wife's birthday present there because he knew she'd never find it.

It's people like them that keep suburban restaurant chains going, but their kids aren't the same.

Country clubs are closing down

No one's taking up golf anymore. That standard pastime of suburban life is under real stress, with over 800 golf courses shutting down across the country in the past decade. People between the ages of eighteen and thirty just aren't interested, which means suburban residential golf estates are in trouble too. Selling houses based on the availability of a practice putting green or lessons with the resident golf pro is less and less successful.

Corporations want a city address

"In the past several years, a handful of America's largest corporations have joined a mass exodus from their suburban headquarters to new home bases in the city, and millennials seem to be the driving force," wrote *Business Insider*'s Chris Weller.[13]

He lists McDonald's, Kraft Heinz, General Electric, and ConAgra Foods as all leaving suburbia in order to headquarter downtown. Swiss bank UBS recently established a New York City headquarters, abandoning Stamford, Connecticut, after fifteen years. According to Chris Weller, the reason was because "UBS realized much of its top talent lived or wanted to live 35 miles south, in Manhattan."[14]

KEEP THE CHURCH WEIRD

In the very early 2000s, the Euclid Square shopping mall in suburban Cleveland went broke. The fountains and escalators were turned off. The stores were all shuttered. Weeds grew in cracks throughout the parking lot. Paint started peeling from the façades. For nearly a decade, Euclid Square was a big, sad, dead mall.

But then, a number of small churches started renting the vacant stores in the 687,000-square-foot shopping center. The Grace and Mercy Church of the Living God rented the old Foot Locker; God's Way Gospel Church took over a Dollar Tree; House of Elohim in Jesus Christ meets in the old Diamond's Men's Shop; Crown of Life is in a Fashion Bug; and Faith Baptist Church took over an empty beauty parlor. At its peak, nearly one-quarter of the 100 empty storefront spaces in Euclid Square was rented for Sunday worship and weekday Bible studies. It was like an ecclesial outlet mall.

The owners of the mall were happy. They got to offer these small congregations reasonable month-to-month leases—$500 to $1,000—on spaces that would have otherwise just been collecting dust. And the churches were happy. They got reasonable rent on some property until they were big enough to buy or rent more permanent facilities.

And presumably potential congregation members were happy too. They could quite conveniently browse the twenty-four churches like they do clothing or furniture stores, giving a whole new meaning to the phrase "church shopping."

But it couldn't last. The small rental return didn't match the cost of maintaining the huge facility, and in 2016, the city of Euclid ordered the owners to close the mall due to safety concerns.

There isn't a more powerful metaphor for the suburban church than the closure of Euclid Square and the eviction of those twenty-four congregations. Baby boomers have so connected church culture to the culture of American suburbia that as suburbia dies, churches are dying with it. Along with the local shopping mall, Outback Steakhouse, and the golf club, we are now routinely talking about the demise of the suburban church. Ed Stetzer reports that 80 to 85 percent of American churches are on the downside of their life cycle, thirty-five hundred to four thousand churches close each year, and the number of unchurched has almost doubled from 1990 to 2004.[15]

It's another reason why we need to keep Christianity weird. Not only for the reasons we looked at in the previous chapter, but because our culture is telling us something about the values of the emerging generation of so-called millennials. They want their church to be weird in many of the same ways Austin or Santa Cruz or Portland are weird because many of those ways mirror biblical values. For them, a weird form of Christianity would include at least the following elements:

Connection to place

Running parallel to the decline of anchor stores and chain restaurants is the growth of localism—farm-to-table restaurants, locally brewed beers, and conspicuous community involvement by locally owned establishments. Set alongside these innovations, a church that seems like a franchise can simultaneously seem like a betrayal of these values. Younger people are leery of churches that have no connection to its immediate place; that isn't engaged in the life of the city that hosts it; that doesn't support local businesses; that isn't concerned with artistic expression and experimentation. There's a desire for a more indigenous, rooted, authentic community of faith to spring up in the soil in which it's planted.

Too many suburban churches are hermetically sealed

boxes, air-conditioned 24–7, with massive parking lots that encourage members to drive from long distances away to attend services. Some of them come equipped with bookstores, coffee shops, and fitness centers. I visited one that had a beauty salon off the foyer. To the generation that loves the Weird Cities doctrine, these kinds of churches are like the religious version of the strip mall or the faux town square.

Alan Roxburgh bemoans that such churches seem to be attempting to "act like vacuum cleaners, sucking people out of their neighborhoods into a sort of Christian supermarket."[16] He continues, urging us to see the importance of locally focused, incarnational missional communities:

> Our culture does not need any more
> churches run like corporations; it needs local
> communities empowered by the gospel vision
> of a transforming Christ who addresses the
> needs of the context and changes the polis into
> a place of hope and wholeness. The corporation
> churches we are cloning across the land cannot
> birth this transformational vision, because they
> have no investment in context or place; they
> are centers of expressive individualism with
> a truncated gospel of personal salvation and
> little else.[17]

Environmental sustainability

Not only are such franchise-model churches out of sync with broader societal currents, they're costly to create and maintain—not only financially but environmentally. Personally, I've attended too many events in suburban churches where I've been served coffee in plastic cups and meals in Styrofoam boxes, with the sandwich, the muffin, and the chips all separately sealed in plastic. The trash cans can't contain the amount of nonbiodegradable packaging that gets thrown out at the end of the event. The generation that is done with Generica is also done with unsustainable practices in the church. Followers of the creator God should be at the forefront of the environmental movement, working toward energy efficiency in their properties and places of worship, teaching and encouraging their members to adopt environmentally sustainable lifestyles as a dimension of their spiritual practice.

And yet a Pew Forum on Religion & Public Life poll found that "only 34% of America's white evangelical Protestants accepted there is solid evidence that global warming is real and that it is attributable to humans."[18] No surprise, the same study revealed that there is a yawning gap between the views of younger and older Christians: "More than half of people under age 30 (54%) believe that the earth is warming mostly because of human activity compared with only 37% of those ages 65 and older."[19]

Doesn't look like the kids are going to have much luck banning high-wattage incandescent light bulbs or getting "no idling" signs installed around the church parking lot. And they can forget about the church buying its energy from green energy sources or providing eco-friendly biocompostable paper products at all their events. Imagine how disorienting it must be for people to be told in every area of life to conserve and reduce their footprint except in church. Is this the kind of counterculture we mean by eccentric? Or is it tone-deafness?

Open to the views of all, especially the marginalized

There's less interest among emerging generations in a form of Christianity in which a handful of people have all the say and the vast majority get to say nothing. Especially when those with all the say are exclusively white men. Emerging generations have been raised on interactive learning methods and social media. They expect to be able to voice their opinions and hear the opinions of others. They want to hear the voices of those who've got nothing to lose by holding those opinions—the outcast, the marginalized, and especially, women's voices. The phenomenal and surprising effectiveness of the recent #MeToo social media movement illustrates this. After decades of ignoring or silencing the voices of women who have routinely experienced sexual harassment and sexual assault in every area of society, the floodgates opened after several high-profile cases came to light. The relatively newfound mantra "believe the victim" illustrates my point. In a similar vein, several high-profile conference speakers and preachers have signed "the panel pledge," a commitment not to present at events at which there is not gender and ethnic diversity in the speaker lineup. It feels like there's a cultural shift toward acknowledging the voiceless and honoring those who have been silenced, as well as a desire to confront issues, even if they are uncomfortable for us.

Churches that don't encourage questions, that can't cope with doubt, or that blanch when the "wrong" thing is said, no matter how tentatively, are increasingly out of step with their culture.

Ethnic diversity

New Testament scholar Scot McKnight has declared, "The church God wants is one brimming with difference." That's the church emerging generations want too. In his book *A Fellowship of Differents*, McKnight continues,

We've made the church into the American
dream for our own ethnic group with the same
set of convictions about next to everything.
No one else feels welcome. What Jesus and the
apostles taught was that you were welcomed
because the church welcomed all to the table.[20]

It's been nearly ten years since theologian Soong-
Chan Rah released *The Next Evangelicalism*, calling for
the church to break free from limiting and exclusive
paradigms and fully embrace the dramatic cultural
diversity that is rapidly defining the twenty-first century in the United States. Sadly, the suburban church
continues to reinforce Martin Luther King's scathing
assessment that eleven o'clock on Sunday morning is
the most segregated hour of the American week.

WEIRD CITIES AREN'T PERFECT

The Weird Cities movement hasn't created completely
safe, perfectly harmonious urban communities. While the
intentions might be good, things in places like Portland
and Austin get spoiled by human greed and self-interest.
For example, Portland currently finds itself in the grip of
clashes between left-wing so-called "antifas" (antifascists)
and white nationalist groups. Protests and counterprotests
are ratchetting up the violence across the city.

Furthermore, weird cities have not been effective in guarding against gentrification, which has only added to preexisting social inequities. Back in the 1990s, social scientists coined the term "food desert" to describe urban and suburban communities where easy access to nutritious food was limited. These were the neighborhoods where you could easily buy junk food at local corner stores and fast-food outlets but getting to a market for fresh fruit and vegetables was a challenge. In response to this, the US government helped raise $1 billion, including $170 million in grants, to end food deserts. They funded new stores and farmers markets. Weird Cities like Portland and Austin embraced the Healthy Food Financing Initiative, providing loans, grants, and tax breaks to grocery stores willing to set up in neighborhoods that qualify as food deserts. Businesses preferred by urban professionals, stores like Whole Foods, Trader Joes, and New Seasons, started popping up in these communities. The food deserts disappeared. Neighborhoods that previously didn't have access to fresh vegetables now had hipster grocery stores selling ten different types of lettuce. At premium prices. Portland is now faced with a more concerning outcome—food mirages. In his alarming article, "The Depressing Truth about Hipster Food Towns," Stephen Tucker Paulsen concluded,

As urban neighborhoods gentrify, a new kind of disparity has emerged. Many experts, including some federal researchers, stress that high local grocery prices—not simply distance—prevent lower-income households from eating well. . . . While "conventionally defined food deserts are rare in Portland," a pair of researchers concluded in a 2013 paper, "food mirages, by contrast, cover much of the city."[21]

We could go on, listing the failed experiments and broken promises of the Weird City movement. These cities tend to wrestle with an exclusivity, a cliquishness, that exiles "normals"—anyone who can't live up to (or afford) the agreed-upon quirkiness. Weird Christianity needs to be contrasted with the kind of privileged weirdness the weird cities promote. The solution to a domesticated Christianity isn't to banish the normal but to affirm and empower the weird. Christian weirdness is not an exclusivity but a kind of hospitality, a making room for eccentricity.

Cities like Portland and a host of others are an expression of yearning—deep yearning—among young people for greater commitment to social justice, community development, responsible business practices, environmentalism, conviviality, and hospitality. And which of those things could Christians say they are not also deeply committed to? When I call on you to keep Christianity weird, I'm asking you to reject materialism, foster community, promote diversity, share resources, protect the environment, start ethical businesses, feed the hungry, play beautiful music, bring peace and joy and life back to our cities. Portland and Austin and Santa Cruz and a hundred cities across America can't do this in and of themselves, but eccentric followers of an eccentric God can lead the way.

FOR YOUR CONSIDERATION

1. Think of a city that is featured in a film or television show you've watched recently. What was weird about that city? What appealed to you about it? What about it made you nervous?

2. Would you characterize the place you live as "conventional" or "crazy"? Why? What would you say are real distinctives of your city?

3. Beyond the zanier aspects of the Weird City movement, which of its values do you find most compelling? Where do you see overlap between its values and Christian values? Where do you see a parting of the ways?

4. What's the difference between being responsive, as a person or community of faith, to the values and priorities of your neighbors and maintaining a distinct Christian witness? How have you seen those two priorities handled well?

JESUS WAS
THE ORIGINAL WEIRDO

Jesus was the original weirdo with a beardo.

T-SHIRT SLOGAN

If you're open to the renewal of your mind by the Holy Spirit, and if such renewal serves the purpose of making us more like Jesus, then you need to brace yourself— you're going to get more weird!

That's because Jesus was the original weirdo.

The Gospel accounts continue to defy the church's best efforts throughout history to turn Jesus into some kind of tame, dignified religious leader. Again and again, the Gospels reveal Jesus to be a strange and unlikely messiah. So strange and unlikely, in fact, that those who were searching the signs most intently for the coming of the promised king completely missed him.

This perspective is presented most powerfully by

Mark's Gospel, which begins in rather dramatic fashion with a wild and crazy John the Baptist, dressed in camel's hair clothing and subsisting on a diet of locusts and wild honey, screaming at his listeners, "After me comes the one more powerful than I, the straps of whose sandals I am not worthy to stoop down and untie. I baptize you with water, but he will baptize you with the Holy Spirit" (Mark 1:7-8).

In other words, "If you think I'm weird, wait until you get a load of the guy who's coming!"

When we do meet that guy, he definitely lives up to John's introduction. In chapter 1 alone, Jesus is baptized under a torn sky and a descending Holy Spirit, is sent out into the wilderness to be with wild beasts while angels ministered to him, and drives out demons and heals all manner of sicknesses. Mark 1 gives the impression of a wild Messiah wandering the highways and byways of Israel accompanied by wild animals and angels and with demons and sickness flying off in every direction.

Soon after, we start to get an impression of how the religious leaders saw him. Not just as weird, but dangerous.

In Mark 2:6-7, he's accused of blasphemy for claiming to be able to forgive sins.

In Mark 2:16, aspersions are cast on him because he is socializing with sinful people and Roman collaborators.

In Mark 2:23-24, he is called a lawbreaker.

In Mark 3:20-21, his own family try to apprehend him because they believe he is insane.

And soon after (Mark 3:22) the teachers of the law interpret his behavior not as insanity, but demon possession. In fact, they believe he is possessed by Beelzebul, the daddy of all demons.

You can't get very far into Mark's Gospel without having to come to terms with the out-and-out strangeness of Jesus.

Years ago, a publisher asked the gothic rock singer-songwriter Nick Cave to write an introduction to Mark's Gospel. At first, Cave was uncertain, recalling Jesus as the "wet, all-loving, etiolated individual" he heard about in his childhood Anglican Church, "the decaf of worship."[1] But to his surprise, the Jesus he discovered in Mark's Gospel wasn't the wishy-washy Christ of his childhood church. It was the wild Messiah. He explains,

> The Christ that emerges from *Mark*, tramping
> through the haphazard events of His life, had
> a ringing intensity about Him that I could not
> resist. . . . The Christ that the Church offers
> us, the bloodless, placid "Saviour"—the man
> smiling benignly at a group of children, or
> calmly, serenely hanging from the cross—denies
> Christ His potent, creative sorrow or His boiling

anger that confronts us so forcefully in *Mark*. Thus the Church denies Christ His humanity, offering up a figure that we can perhaps "praise" but never relate to. The essential humanness of *Mark*'s Christ provides us with a blueprint for our own lives, so that we have something we can aspire to, rather than revere, that can lift us free of the mundanity of our existences, rather than affirming the notion that we are lowly and unworthy.[2]

As we explored in the previous chapter, if the renewal of the mind by the Holy Spirit opens our eyes to the gospel and shapes us to become more like Jesus, then it follows that we, too, should become more weird the more Christlike we become. Nick Cave concludes,

Merely to praise Christ in His Perfectness, keeps us on our knees, with our heads pitifully bent. Clearly, this is not what Christ had in mind. Christ came as a liberator. Christ understood that we as humans were for ever held to the ground by the pull of gravity— our ordinariness, our mediocrity—and it was through His example that He gave our imaginations the freedom to rise and to fly. In short, to be Christ-like.[3]

I sometimes despair at the advice given to Christians by some of their teachers and leaders, cautioning them not to be weird. Be different, they say, but don't be a nut. Don't be strange. But any cursory reading of the Gospels reveals Jesus to be very strange, even to his strongest supporters and closest friends.

He was a homeless, unmarried, thirtysomething rabbi who recruited a bunch of young (some still in their teens), uneducated boys to hit the road with him, preaching the coming of the Kingdom and calling on people to repent of their sins.

He didn't mince words. He told the truth, even when it made people hate him. Especially when it made powerful people hate him.

He fraternized with prostitutes, extortionists, collaborators, zealots, and those euphemistically referred to as "sinners"—ordinary, irreligious people. He was unconcerned by what his friendship with such people would suggest to others.

When he taught people, he didn't quote directly from the Torah. While he did refer to "the Law of Moses, the Prophets and the Psalms" (as in Luke 24:44, for example), he didn't do so as normal religious teachers, which was to provide commentary on specific ancient texts. On the one occasion when he came closest to doing so, in Luke 4 where he reads Isaiah 61:1-2 and announces, "Today this scripture is fulfilled in your hearing," it literally caused a riot.

Instead of telling stories about Moses or Abraham, he told them about housewives, farmers, business managers, and disrespectful sons. To describe his vision of the Kingdom, he referred to yeast and seeds, a mustard bush, a pearl, a banquet. None of this sounded to the casual observer like normal religious teaching at all.[4]

He was a miracle worker. He could read minds. He knew when people thought ill of him and when they would betray him.

Only the guileless—simple fishermen, lepers, outsiders, the sick, the possessed—felt at home around him. The conspiratorial, the proud, those with much to lose—they despised him, because he knew too much and what he knew could bring their worlds crashing down around them.

What he asked of them was that they repent. All he wanted was for them to move out of the shadows, away from their guile, their scheming, their fear, and into the light. His light.

Get real, he demanded. Repent. Quit lying to yourself. Love one another. Do good.

To some he met, he was absolutely weird. To others, he was beautifully winsome. It all depended on whether you wanted freedom. Jesus came, bringing the weird and winsome message that you can be truly free if you follow him. He personifies what we looked at in chapter 1. He possessed the kind of cognitive disinhibition of the eccentric identified by Shelly Carson. If the renewal of the mind by the Holy Spirit makes us more like Jesus, it will make us weirder and more winsome, just like him. Here are a few case studies as proof.

WINSOME AND WEIRD CASE STUDY 1: NICODEMUS

Most Christians know the story of Jesus' encounter with the Pharisee Nicodemus in John 3. Their conversation gave rise to one of the best-known verses in the Bible—John 3:16. But don't let your familiarity with the words "For God so loved the world . . ." cause you to overlook how remarkably weird Jesus' interaction with Nicodemus was.

A visit from a guy like Nicodemus might normally be considered a big deal, even if he did arrive furtively under the cover of darkness. John introduces him as "a Pharisee, . . . a member of the Jewish ruling council" (John 3:1), which is really saying something. He was religious (a Pharisee), educated (Nicodemus is a Greek name), and powerful (a ruler). Most importantly, he was a son of Abraham, a guardian of the Jewish tradition, and he begins his meeting with Jesus by saying, "Rabbi, we know that you are a teacher who has come from God. For no one could perform the signs you are doing if God were not with him" (verse 2). That's his way of saying, "Bro, I'm a son of Abraham, a child of God, and I know you are too." It's a statement of solidarity.

But Jesus wasn't having any of it.

His reply is downright strange, if not rude. "Very truly I tell you, no one can see the kingdom of God unless they are born again" (verse 3).

He's basically saying, "Dude, don't think we're brothers just because we share the same bloodline. To join my family, you must be born again." Or maybe more accurately, "born from above," because one of Jesus' best-known expressions, "to be born again," might not be best translated that way. There's actually some ambiguity in the Greek text: *anōthen* generally means "from above, from on high," although it can refer to repetition, hence "again" or "anew."

Actually, it might be intended to mean both. In the context of Jesus' conversation with a proud Jewish leader like Nicodemus, and given what he tells him later about fleshly birth and spiritual birth, it seems clear he is telling the Pharisee that his physical birth in the line of Abraham isn't enough for him to enter the Kingdom of God. He needs another birth, a spiritual birth from above.

This isn't just a strange esoteric answer. To someone like Nicodemus, it would have been utterly offensive.

You see, all Jews, but especially religious ones like Nicodemus, believed their descent from Abraham guaranteed their entry into heaven. A common image often painted by rabbis at the time was that of Abraham standing watch at the gates of hell ensuring none of his children accidentally entered there.[5] Now, here was another rabbi, one whose miraculous powers assured Nicodemus he must be from God, daring to teach that their physical birth as Jews was no such guarantee at all. They must be born from above.

It says something about the strength of his curiosity about Jesus that Nicodemus stays and continues the conversation. He replies, "Huh?"

Seriously, that's pretty much his answer. He has no clue what Jesus is talking about. I've heard preachers saying that Nicodemus' inability to grasp what Jesus was saying was indicative of his sinful heart, but let's face it, "You must be born from above" is pretty cryptic teaching. What exactly does it mean to be born from above? Here's Jesus' explanation:

> Very truly I tell you, no one can enter the
> kingdom of God unless they are born of water
> and the Spirit. Flesh gives birth to flesh, but
> the Spirit gives birth to spirit. You should not
> be surprised at my saying, "You must be born
> again." The wind blows wherever it pleases.

You hear its sound, but you cannot tell where
it comes from or where it is going. So it is with
everyone born of the Spirit.

JOHN 3:5-8

In brief, he's saying that those who are born of the
Spirit are free! They are disinhibited in the way that
the wind is disinhibited. Collective behavior no longer
constrains them. To the outside observer, they probably
appear eccentric, but that's because they are—and their
eccentricity, birthed in them by the eccentric God, has
set them free.

Nicodemus and his compatriots are trapped within
the confines of their fleshly birth, their bloodlines, their
heritage, and their religious system. You are anchored to
the earth, Nicodemus, but if you could be born from
above you would be free indeed.

Bear all this in mind and jump over to John 10 with
me. Jesus isn't speaking to Nicodemus any longer, but
he is talking to Nicodemus's crew, the Pharisees. And his
condemnation of the Pharisees in John 10 should be seen
as the background to his conversation with Nicodemus
the Pharisee in chapter 3.

In John 10, the metaphor isn't birth, but shepherd-
ing. He begins,

Very truly I tell you Pharisees, anyone who does
not enter the sheep pen by the gate, but climbs
in by some other way, is a thief and a robber.
The one who enters by the gate is the shepherd
of the sheep. The gatekeeper opens the gate for
him, and the sheep listen to his voice. He calls
his own sheep by name and leads them out.
When he has brought out all his own, he goes on
ahead of them, and his sheep follow him because
they know his voice. But they will never follow
a stranger; in fact, they will run away from him
because they do not recognize a stranger's voice.

JOHN 10:1-5

We often confuse what Jesus is saying here and think
he means as a good shepherd, it's his task to keep the
sheep safe inside the sheep pen. Actually, he's saying the
opposite. He's condemning the Pharisees for penning
the people of Israel within their draconian religious laws
and teaching that God's Kingdom is for Jews alone. Not
so, says Jesus! He calls his own sheep by name and leads
them out.

No sheep wants to be locked in a dry, dusty sheep
pen. They want to graze in green pastures beside fresh
streams. And Jesus is saying he's come to lead them to
freedom, away from the earthly control of Israel's leaders.
And then, in verse 16, he says the weirdest thing.

I have other sheep that are not of this sheep
pen. I must bring them also. They too will
listen to my voice, and there shall be one
flock and one shepherd.

The gift of the Kingdom of God was entrusted
to Israel in order that they take it to the nations and
invite Gentiles to come under the reign of Yahweh
and find life. Instead, the Pharisees had closed ranks.
They had shuttered Israel from the outside world and
refused entry to Gentiles unless they undertook the
most daunting process of conversion. Jesus tells them
he has come to satisfy God's covenant with Israel and to
lead his people to freedom, to join with those non-Jews
who would acknowledge the Good Shepherd and unite
them as a new, spiritual nation under his kingship.

Remember back in chapter 1, I quoted Richard
Beck saying the Kingdom of Jesus is eccentric because it
doesn't create walls or borders; it is "embedded, pilgrim,
landless, possessionless, homeless, sojourning, itinerant [and] missionary."[6] Here is Jesus being his most
eccentric.

And just like Nicodemus in chapter 3, the Pharisees
are dumbstruck and have no idea what Jesus is talking
about (John 10:6).

This, I believe, sheds more light on that strange conversation Jesus has with Nicodemus. To be born of the

Spirit, or born from above, is to be set free from the earthbound burden of your Jewish birth. It means being set free from religious legalism and superiority and being lifted up from earth and scattered by the Spirit to the four corners of the planet to bring the Good News of the Kingdom to all.

In his beautiful book *The Spirituals and the Blues*, James Cone says that slaves and the children of slaves used spirituals to express exactly this idea. Though literally enslaved, this music affirmed their spiritual freedom and their essential humanity in the face of oppression. Though physically born slaves, they had been born from above, and this gave them a new sense of dignity in light of the promises of God. While their slave owners defined them as nothing, the spirituals redefined a powerful sense of black identity and hope. For slaves, their Christian music became a medium for lifting them up from their physical state and reshaping them by their extraordinary eschatological hope.

The only ones unnerved by their singing should have been the slave owners. In the same way, the only ones unnerved by Jesus' teaching were the Pharisees. They were like slave owners, trying desperately to maintain their system of control. As we've seen, prostitutes, lepers, tax collectors, and outsiders were profoundly drawn to Jesus' message of freedom. They needed to be born from above, because the promises of their fleshly birth had been well and truly dashed.

To be born again, then, isn't simply to embrace a certain set of doctrinal beliefs about human sin and the atonement of Christ. It means to be free. Truly free. In Christ. As James Cone says elsewhere, "Any theology that is indifferent to the theme of liberation is not Christian theology."[7]

Nicodemus is intrigued by all this. And asks the most obvious question—"How?"

How does one experience this rebirth from above?

And then things get even weirder.

Jesus refers to an obscure (and frankly, odd) story buried back in Numbers 21, where the Israelites, wandering in the wilderness, are afflicted by nests of poisonous snakes. Moses is told by God to make a bronze serpent and elevate it on a pole so that if anyone is bitten by a snake, they only have to look at it and they'll be healed.

We all know what Jesus means, right? After all, we've read to the end of the story. We know he will be lifted up on a "pole" as he suffers and dies for our sins. We know what he means by his reference to Numbers 21, but how could Nicodemus understand? It must have been the strangest conversation. But as we've seen and will continue to see, strange conversations with Jesus were par for the course.

WINSOME AND WEIRD CASE STUDY 2:
THE BLEEDING WOMAN

The Gospel writers often take great care in recording the names of individual *men* Jesus met (Nicodemus, Zacchaeus, Bartimaeus, Jairus), but not the women. Our second weird encounter with Jesus is one of the Gospels' most beautiful, but the female protagonist is sadly unnamed, known only throughout history as the hemorrhaging or bleeding woman.

The nameless woman's story appears in all three synoptic Gospels (Matthew 9:20-22; Mark 5:25-34; Luke 8:43-48) and constitutes one of Jesus' strangest and yet most touching miracles.

In all three accounts, the healing of the bleeding woman is presented as an interruption to a larger story—Jesus raising Jairus's daughter from the dead. Jairus, a synagogue leader, has approached Jesus, asking him to heal his dying child, and the two of them, together with the disciples, are making their way through a dense crowd of onlookers and supplicants toward Jairus's house. En route, the nameless woman approaches Jesus in secret, blending in with the thronging crowd, believing if she can merely touch the fringe of Jesus' cloak, she might be healed.

The Gospel writers tell us she had been subject to vaginal bleeding for twelve years. She had spent all her money on remedies and treatments, only to find herself destitute and alone, a shadow person dwelling at the edges of society. She would have been viewed as a *niddah*, that is, a menstruating woman, and therefore ceremonially unclean. But she wasn't menstruating. She was continuously bleeding, which effectively made her a permanent niddah, in a constant state of uncleanness. The implications of this are tragic. At this time, no man would put up with this condition. As a single woman, a very rare thing, she lived an extremely tenuous existence in the ancient Near East. It would appear she was unable to carry a child or give birth. She would have been barred entry to the synagogue or temple. She was broke.

I can't emphasize enough the social and religious isolation she—an unmarried, childless, penniless woman, unable to enter religious premises or make offerings to God—would have endured, not to mention the discomfort of her physical condition.

Little wonder she believes she can't approach Jesus directly.

Instead, she tries to steal a miracle from him by touching the fringe of his garment.

At first, this might seem like an odd decision, but there was some precedent for this decision. The Pharisees at that time had taken to wearing the *tzitzit*—extra-long fringes or tassels on their prayer shawls or clothing. In Matthew 23:5, Jesus berates them for such outward displays of religiosity, bemoaning, "They make their phylacteries wide and the tassels on their garments long." Nonetheless, common people had come to believe that because of the Pharisees' great religious standing, their tzitzit was imbued with a mystical power.[8] This might very well be exactly what the Pharisees wanted them to think, but Jesus had scorned them for behaving so. There's no power in a Pharisee's tzitzit whatsoever, he declares. It's all for show. They're charlatans.

Unaware of this, and assuming Jesus to be equivalent to a Pharisee, the bleeding woman comes to believe that if she could just touch the fringe of his clothing, she would be healed.

This whole situation is so desperately sad. A filthy, hungry, sick woman, who dares not appear openly in public or approach a holy man face-to-face, slinks furtively through the crowd, edging her way toward Jesus, not knowing there's actually no special power in the fringe of his robe.

And yet . . .

Mark's Gospel says that upon touching Jesus' cloak, "Immediately her bleeding stopped and she felt in her body that she was freed from her suffering" (Mark 5:29).

It's weird, isn't it?

Even though Jesus isn't a Pharisee and the fringe of his cloak isn't magic, this poor, forlorn woman has reached out in faith, and that is all it takes.

Remember, Jesus was being led by Jairus toward his home and his dying daughter. Did he see the woman approach? Did he know what was in her mind? Did he recognize her plan was misguided, even if her faith in him was well placed? Or was the whole miracle a surprise to him, as suggested by what he said next?

> At once Jesus realized that power had gone out from him. He turned around in the crowd and asked, "Who touched my clothes?"
>
> "You see the people crowding against you," his disciples answered, "and yet you can ask, 'Who touched me?'"
>
> But Jesus kept looking around to see who had done it.
>
> MARK 5:30-32

It seems so unlikely that Jesus was ignorant of what had happened, as if you could trick him into healing you unawares. I might be wrong, but I've always assumed he knew exactly what had happened and he had honored the woman's mistaken belief in the mystical quality of his fringe because behind that belief was a deep faith in him as her Savior. I suspect he is feigning surprise and calling on the identity of the miracle thief in order to do precisely what he does next:

Then the woman, knowing what had happened
to her, came and fell at his feet and, trembling
with fear, told him the whole truth.

MARK 5:33

He forced the terrified woman, accustomed as she was
to the shadows, to step out into an assembly of men and
to testify to her actions. He did it, though, not to shame
her, but to honor her.

He said to her, "Daughter, your faith has healed
you. Go in peace and be freed from your suffering."

MARK 5:34

In the assembly of men, in the presence of a synagogue
leader, Jesus brings testimony of the bloodied woman's
great faith. He makes her the hero. He's doing what he
told Nicodemus he would do. He's being the ultimate
eccentric, leading his sheep out of darkness and fear, out
of religious superstition and sickness, into fresh pastures.

WINSOME AND WEIRD CASE STUDY 3:
THE CHILDREN IN THE TEMPLE

Most people are familiar with the story of Jesus fashioning a whip of cords and driving the money changers out
of the Temple, scattering their coins and overturning

their tables. He was infuriated by the ecclesial trade that had sprung up at that time that allowed worshipers to purchase sacrificial animals and change their foreign coins right in the Temple precincts.

Jews and proselytes had traveled from far and wide for the annual Passover festival and needed to exchange their Roman currency, which bore the head of the godlike emperor Caesar, for shekels in order to pay the temple tax.

They also needed to offer animal sacrifices, but, having traveled far from home, would have no such animal with them. This had encouraged dealers in cattle and sheep to set up in an outer court of the Temple— in every likelihood the Court of the Gentiles—and charge premium prices for animals. And those who sold pigeons to the poor (those unable to afford a sheep) would do likewise.

The animal dealers and money changers had the international visitors over a barrel. It was worshiper exploitation. And Jesus was outraged:

> "It is written," he said to them, "'My house will be called a house of prayer,' but you are making it 'a den of robbers.'"
>
> MATTHEW 21:13

A lot of people have assumed that Jesus was motivated primarily by concern that the hallowed halls of the

Jewish Temple were being defiled by the tawdry business of religious trade. But remember, earlier I mentioned his words to the Pharisees about being the Good Shepherd who leads his sheep out to green pastures and how he wishes to call sheep from other pens to join them (John 10). It was these very sheep—the ones from "other pens"—who were being disadvantaged by the trade in religious devotion going on in the Temple. The Pharisees who had restricted the news of God's Kingdom to the geographic borders of Israel were also restricting worship of that God to those who could pay for animals and currency exchange.

In "cleansing the Temple"—as this incident is often called—Jesus reinforces his promise to set God's people free and to unite them with Gentile believers, whom he would call from other nations. It is an overt act of religious rebellion.

But it's what happens next that makes the hair stand up on the back of my neck.

Matthew reports that once the court was vacated by the money changers, the blind and the lame came to him, and he healed them (Matthew 21:14). The verse says they "came to him," but they may have already been there, begging for alms from worshipers, and perhaps when Jesus drove everyone out, they remained, unable to leave so easily. But it gives the impression that after Jesus created a void in the Temple, the space was filled up with the most broken and needy people. And as Jesus healed them all, the most unlikely choir filled the temple with song. Children—possibly the children of the money changers or even the blind and lame themselves—burst into praise: "Hosanna to the Son of David" (verse 15).

This strange and improbable Messiah is left alone in his "Father's house," as he called it (John 2:16), surrounded by children and the disabled. These were the days when both those categories were silent in general society, their voices unacknowledged, unheard.

The dancing, cavorting, laughter, and singing of Jerusalem street urchins forms the most adorable act of worship recorded in Scripture.

And of course, the chief priests and the teachers of the law stood at a distance, disgusted with what they observed, unable to see in this beautiful scene both the fulfillment of Scripture and the weird new world Jesus was ushering in.

Yep, Jesus was pretty strange. But it's in his weirdness that Jesus reveals more than just what an eccentric lifestyle looks like. He reveals the folly of the world as it is. New Testament scholar James Resseguie describes Jesus' use of opaque language and unlikely metaphors and how strange it made Jesus appear to his contemporaries. But he goes further, saying that Jesus' teaching and language reinforces not only his own otherness but also shows up the outlandishness of the assertions of the dominant culture. Resseguie says, "It is true that his forms of speech emphasize *his strangeness*, but his strangeness serves to emphasize *our strangeness*, making strange our common, narcotized way of viewing the world."[9]

Here is the weird and winsome example of Jesus: At first, he seems strange to us, but the more we look, the more we realize that what is really strange is the culture in which we have become content. We have been sleepwalking. But the strangeness of Jesus wakes us up to the world as it should be.

FOR YOUR CONSIDERATION

1. What was your initial reaction to the title of this chapter, "Jesus Was the Original Weirdo"? Were you intrigued? Offended? Why?

2. Which of the "weird and winsome case studies" offers the most appealing portrait of Jesus for you? Why?

3. How might a similar encounter play out today in the churches in your community? What do you think Jesus would say to your church? Why? In what ways do you think churches have "domesticated" Jesus, making him safer and less confronting than the Gospels depict him?

4. How do you think our churches can recapture the
   biblical Jesus, in all his winsomeness and weirdness?

4

BEFORE WE BECAME CONVENTIONAL

Take from the church the miraculous, the supernatural,
the incomprehensible, the unreasonable, the impossible, the
unknowable, and the absurd, and nothing but a vacuum remains.

ROBERT G. INGERSOLL

Before we became conventional, the Christian movement was considered fundamentally out of sync with the powers and principalities that occupy a fallen world. The Christian movement from the beginning was an alternative, redeemed society. It was considered so odd, it continually confounded those around them. The church at its best is always weird. But more than being socially odd, the church has always championed uncommon causes. Priorities only recently taken up by the Weird Cities movement—social justice, community development, responsible business practices, environmentalism, conviviality, community, and the like—have always been Christian priorities. So any call to keep Christianity weird should have the emphasis on the word *keep*. At our best, we are weird, and this has been proven throughout history.

THE HISTORICAL WEIRDNESS OF THE CHURCH

In his final book, *The Patient Ferment of the Early Church*, Alan Kreider examined the first 400 years of the church's history, in order to figure out, "Why did this minor mystery religion from the eastern Mediterranean—marginal, despised, discriminated against—grow substantially, eventually supplanting the well-endowed, respectable cults that were supported by the empire and aristocracy?"[1]

What he found was that, far from the common view that the church grew like a wildfire across the empire, the people of God slowly and patiently fostered the conditions that turned them into a force that could not be contained. According to Kreider, three fundamental ways they did this included (1) embodying a patient eschatological hope, trusting in what God had said about the future, (2) committing themselves to countercultural communal practices or habits, and (3) discipling newcomers via a formal catechesis and alternative worship.[2]

This is so different from the way we're taught to grow the church today, when there seems to be a new evangelistic strategy coming at us every month. Kreider says the early church focused their attention not on strategies, but on habits, prayer, teaching, and worship. They trusted that God was at work in the world, lived in radical obedience to Jesus, and shaped an alternative lifestyle that intrigued and attracted outsiders.

In other words, the earliest Christians taught themselves to be weird like Jesus and created habitual practices to help keep that weirdness in place. This is important. The "patient ferment" Kreider is talking about involves a new kind of discipleship, one that focuses not on strategies or outcomes but on learning and habits. They were fostering the conditions for the "renewing of the mind by the Holy Spirit" we talked about earlier. And getting these conditions embedded into the life of a believer takes time.

Kreider observed that the early church didn't make it easy for newcomers to join, and they certainly didn't ease off once you'd become a member. The church instituted a rigorous form of *catechesis*, a program of spiritual formation and theological instruction carried out in preparation for baptism, lasting up to several years. They also fostered an alternative (for the time) form of worship, centering especially on prayer and food, the focus of which became the celebration of Communion.

Kreider explains that by the end of their lengthy

catechesis, something profound had occurred to the new believers:

> [They] had encountered visions of new life and
> bodily actions that enticed them and stretched
> them into ways of behaving that at times they
> found uncomfortable. They wondered: could
> they become the kind of persons in thought and
> reflex that they were catechized to be? Could
> they embody the Christians' habitus? As they
> struggled with these questions, and as their
> thinking and behavior gradually changed,
> the catechumens learned patience.[3]

Following baptism, the patient ferment of the early believers continued to bubble away. The new habits instilled in their lives "formed the character of the Christians, aligning them with God's purposes and habituating them to the surprising ways of Christ's church."[4]

All that to say, making someone weird like Jesus is a slow, deliberate process. The renewal of the mind doesn't happen all at once in some cataclysmic supernatural experience. It takes time, discipline, a devotion to study, and the adoption of new habits.

In other words, weirdness is not the absence of controls or discipline. True weirdness—Jesus-like weirdness—is so contrary to our natural impulses and interests that embracing it requires focus, patience, and discipline. Lowering your threshold of collective behavior should be an unhurried, methodical process. We need more Christians to be committed to this endeavor, to do as we said at the beginning and "think different," break the rules, disturb the status quo. But not in some undisciplined, chaotic sense.

Vincent van Gogh is widely known today as a thoroughly eccentric artist. He might not have invented impressionism, but he was the first to paint stars swirling uncontrollably in the night sky, or to depict sunflowers as golden explosions, or the sky on fire above a wheat field. His pictures were vivid, wild, daring, chaotic, full of bright yellows and deep blues. If you've ever had the opportunity to visit the Van Gogh Museum in Amsterdam and be surrounded by a room full of his work—*Sunflowers*, *Irises*, *Almond Blossom*, *The Bedroom*, and *The Potato Eaters*—you'll know the powerful visceral effect it can have.

And yet, if you go to the "Van Gogh Close Up" exhibit on the second floor, you can look at van Gogh's early drawings. Collected in drawers you'll find scores of meticulous drawings of hands and feet made by Vincent when he was learning art. And then it dawns on you— Vincent didn't simply pick up a brush and start painting *A Starry Night*. First, he submitted himself to the slow discipline of learning his craft.

Another eccentric artist, Pablo Picasso, once said, "Learn the rules like a pro, so you can break them like an artist." In fact, "breaking the rules like an artist" requires that you first learn those rules carefully. All the grand masters submitted themselves to their craft. They learned the rules before they dared break them. Artist Alexander McQueen once said, "You've got to know the rules to break them. That's what I'm here for, to demolish the rules but to keep the tradition."[5] It's the ability to keep the tradition while breaking the rules that makes all the difference.

I remember my father moaning about modern art and saying anyone could paint like Picasso ("It's just cubes") or Pollock ("You just splash paint on a canvas"). But you try. Your paint splashes on a canvas won't be anywhere near as sublime as Jackson Pollock's.

I think it's the same when it comes to Christian discipleship. The church needs innovators. We need more rule-breakers. But we need the kind of rule-breakers who have taken the long, slow, painful time to learn the rules that need breaking and how to keep the tradition at the same time.

Before you think keeping Christianity weird is a call for wild and carefree rule-breaking, think again. All the great Christian rule-breakers of history submitted themselves to rigorous instruction and discipline as part of their journey into eccentricity. Let's look at a few important movements.

THE HIBERNO-SCOTTISH MISSIONARIES (SIXTH CENTURY)

You might not have heard of the term *Hiberno-Scottish missionaries*. Often, they're referred to simply as the Celts. You might have heard of a few of their leading lights, though—St. Columba of Iona, or St. Aidan of Lindisfarne, or St. Columbanus of the Franks. They were Gaelic monks from Ireland (in Latin: *Hibernia*) and the western coast of modern-day Scotland, who re-Christianized Britain and Western Europe after the fall of Rome. They were wild men from a wild land who harnessed their considerable passions and energies into Christian devotion.

Columba (ca. 521–597) was an Irish nobleman and soldier who became wracked by remorse at causing a battle where many men were slain. He vowed, at the age of thirty-two, to win for Christ as many pagans as Christians whose deaths he had caused. In order to fulfill his vow, he set off with twelve followers for Iona, an isolated island off the southwest coast of Scotland, where he established a monastery-village. There, he re-created the kind of catechism Alan Kreider wrote about, a combination of teaching and habitual practice designed to shape his community into the type of patient mission-ary force not seen since the earliest Christians.

Ultimately, his influence led not only to the Christianizing of Scotland and Britain but also to evan-gelizing as far afield as Germany, France, Italy, and even Africa. He out-debated the Druids, and converted the kings of the Picts and of the Scots. He subjected his fiery Irish temper to the habit of gentleness and love. In so doing, he earned the beautiful nickname "the Dove." He was known everywhere for his love of nature and for his love of God and all people.

Rather than undergoing complete personality trans-plants, the Hiberno-Scots disciplined their passions without extinguishing them. They retained their sense of rowdiness and their love of wild, elemental places like the coastline of Scotland and northern England. They har-nessed their love of drinking and singing and storytelling and directed it toward God. They practiced hospitality, welcoming all comers. They were deeply shaped by their newfound triune faith and saw the Trinity not only as a doctrine but as a framework for all human interactions, highly valuing community, reconciliation, and partner-ship. As a result, their monasteries weren't the cold stone castles of the later medieval period but Christian villages, places of agriculture and study, safety and conviviality.

But they were missionaries, remember. When the abbot, or leader of a monastery, considered certain monks to be ready for missionary service—after years of learning and habit-forming—they would be sent out to take the gospel to the lost. This was done in a most bizarre fashion. All the Hiberno-Scottish monasteries were located on islands or coastlands or at the mouths of rivers. The missionary monks were commissioned by their village and placed in a coracle—a small, circular boat made of wickerwork, covered with a watertight material—and pushed out from shore with the prayer that the Lord of the wind and the waves would take them to the very people He wanted them to save. Coracles were used by fisherman at the time and were propelled with a paddle, but the missionary monks were given no such implement. They were entirely at the mercy of the wind and the tides. Wherever they ran aground, be it Frisia, the Frankish kingdom, or the land of the Norsemen, that was where they were to commence their missionary work of brokering peace, preaching the gospel, and founding monastery-villages like the ones from which they'd come.

They were fearless, dynamic, disciplined, and compassionate missionary wild men. George Hunter suggests we can learn at least three things from the Hiberno-Scottish missionaries:

1. They found a way of connecting their message to the deepest concerns of their listeners. They

helped them see how their feelings matter to the triune God of Christianity;

2. Their experience of God's providence gave them victory over terror and other destructive emotions;

3. Christianity gave them outlets for expressing their constructive emotions through indigenous oratory, storytelling, poetry, music, and dance in God's service.[6]

And they saved Europe. Quite literally. From the darkness of constant war, bloodshed, superstition, and disease, Europe slowly emerged to re-embrace Christianity and forge a new era of Christendom.

THE CISTERCIANS [ELEVENTH CENTURY]

The Celts had landed in pagan Europe in order to re-Christianize a thoroughly post-Christian empire. But by the eleventh century, Europe had been unified under Charlemagne's Holy Roman Empire (later known as the Carolingian Empire), and Christianity was once again the official imperial religion. All the worst excesses of their imperial status—political power, material wealth, military might, and more—began to overcome the church. The parish system became entrenched as a way for the state to financially support the church, and later to fund religious wars. The First Crusade was launched in 1096, beginning a woeful period of church-sponsored violence at the edges of the empire. The greatest challenge facing the church was no longer paganism; it was nominalism.

Around this time, a group of French Benedictine monks became deeply disillusioned with such nominalism. Even within their own order, they detected a relaxation in the observance of the Rule of St. Benedict, instituted by their founder. Uncertain how to push society back toward a deeper devotion to Christ, and frustrated with many of their fellow monks, they decided to withdraw to live a solitary life at Cîteaux (Latin: *Cistercium*), near Dijon, France. There they resolved to live under the strictest interpretation of the Rule of St. Benedict. That meant they embraced a severe form of asceticism. They also refused to accept any feudal revenues, believing it to be sullied by the church's collusion with the state. And they introduced manual labor for monks, making it a principal feature of their common life and the primary means of their financial support. They took seriously the forty-eighth chapter of the Rule of St. Benedict, which states, "For then are they monks in truth, if they live by the work of their hands." As a result, the Cistercians became known for their motto, *Ora et labora*—Pray and Work.

You might have thought a retreatist group of

hardcore monks (and later, nuns) who embraced self-denial and hard work wouldn't have exactly been the flavor of the month in the Middle Ages, but think again. This was a time when the church was mired with the crippling expenses of the Crusades and a massive building program, with huge (and costly) Romanesque cathedrals popping up across the Continent. Any young person with the slightest devotion to Christ knew the only place where that devotion could be fostered and encouraged was among the Cistercians.

Then, in the very early 1100s, a young monk named Bernard (1090–1153) was sent from Cîteaux to establish a Cistercian monastery at Clairvaux. Bernard had been born into Burgundian aristocracy and his regal background, his religious devotion, and his remarkable strength of character effectively made Clairvaux the center of the Cistercian movement. Under his leadership, the order grew spectacularly. No other religious body was increased so greatly in so brief a time. By his death, Bernard had directly founded 68 monasteries from Clairvaux and overseen the establishment of another 270 monasteries from Sweden to Portugal and from Scotland to the countries of the eastern Mediterranean.

In its heyday, the Cistercians were the weirdest monks of all. Europe was used to warrior monks who loved their food and ale (think of the later fictional character

Friar Tuck), but the Cistercians were lean, disciplined, hardworking, and peaceful. They reclaimed unwanted or marginal land and worked it tirelessly, becoming in effect a large, disciplined, unpaid labor force. They were also free from the tariffs and taxes imposed by feudal lords. This made their business enterprises—whether wheat or wool or beer—remarkably profitable, which helped finance the founding of even more monasteries. They're credited with contributing to the whole economic boom of the twelfth century because of their developments in farming techniques, hydraulic engineering, and metallurgy.

Of course, as their wealth and their influence grew, and as their founders and early leaders passed away, the Cistercians themselves fell victim to the temptations of greed and power. Their slide is a good reminder that the basic disciplines of the Christian life aren't just simplicity and industriousness, or even just prayer and Bible study. They include the discipline of being different, which entails considering everything from the seemingly sacred to the seemingly secular through the filter of how it fits in the eccentric Kingdom of God.

Nonetheless, for about a hundred years, these strange monks were about the only ones championing the cause of Christ and providing a flickering flame of truth and life in the midst of Europe's dark centuries.

THE ANABAPTISTS (SIXTEENTH CENTURY)

By the sixteenth century, all the early fears of the Cistercians were fulfilled. The corruption of the church-at-large was widespread and well entrenched. The church's reputation was tarnished by opulence, war, simony (the selling of church offices), nepotism, and internal power struggles (at one point in the late 1300s and 1400s, the church was ruled by three popes simultaneously). Early reformers like John Wycliffe and Jan Hus had met with a grisly end. The religious hegemony ruled with an iron grip.

Most Protestants know something of the history of the Reformation, of Martin Luther nailing his Ninety-Five Theses to the Wittenberg church door in 1517, or of the emergence of John Calvin in Geneva and Ulrich Zwingli in Basel. But less widely known is the story of the Radical Reformation, the second wave of reformers, the sons and daughters of the original reformers, who believed their fathers had been too restrained. They wanted the Reformation to go further, to not only institute a theological or ecclesial revolution but to turn the world upside down. Luther might have reformed the church, but the radical reformers thought European society should be reformed too. They wanted to eliminate the priesthood; abandon infant baptism (which had become a de facto kind of European birth registration); undo the parish system; abolish the privileges of the nobility, cardinals, and popes; offer civil and human rights to all people; and distribute wealth to everyone who had need. They were trouble with a capital T.

While some radical reformers chose the road of violent insurrection, for the most part, they were pacifists, known eventually by the name *Anabaptist*, which means "rebaptizer," because of their practice of baptizing adult converts. For this practice of baptizing adult converts, they were punished with death by drowning, a cruel irony perpetrated by their enemies.

You might not think the way you practice the sacraments would get you into that much trouble, but when the Anabaptists refused to accept your baptism as an infant, this was seen as tantamount to not recognizing you as a European citizen. Indeed, by repudiating their own first baptisms, they were effectively renouncing their citizenship. And they knew it. They saw themselves as citizens of God's Kingdom, not of this world. As noncitizens, they refused to take oaths, join the military, or participate in civil government. Neither the religious nor the secular empires could cope with that. Europe's rulers, fearing an uprising of the lower classes, hounded all Anabaptists as insurrectionists. They were persecuted mercilessly. As one of the founders of the movement, Conrad Grebel, wrote in 1524, "True

Christian believers are sheep among wolves, sheep for the slaughter. . . . Neither do they use worldly sword or war, since all killing has ceased with them."[7] In other words, a movement of pacifist insurrectionists was no match for the might of European lords.

One of the most famous Anabaptists was Menno Simons, a Dutch priest who had broken from the church and joined the outlawed movement in 1536. For the next twenty-five years, he and his family lived as fugitives, evading capture by hiding among supporters.

Charles V offered one hundred guilders for Menno's capture, banned reading of his books and pamphlets, and made it illegal to aid and abet him or his family. Harboring the Simons family attracted a heavy penalty. For sheltering him, one man was broken on the wheel. Transporting Menno along the Meuse River cost one ferryman his life. As Dan Graves wrote, "To know Menno Simons was dangerous; to befriend him, deadly."[8]

His wife and two of his children died during these years on the run. Menno himself suffered physically, and while he avoided capture, he spent his final years hobbling on a crutch. He died in 1561, having eluded capture to the end.

In 1539, twenty-two years prior to his death, Simons wrote a book to answer those critics who insisted he give up and turn himself in, aptly titled *Why I Do Not Cease Teaching and Writing*. He wrote,

True evangelical faith is of such a nature that
it cannot lie dormant, but spreads itself out in
all kinds of righteousness and fruits of love;
it dies to flesh and blood; it destroys all lusts
and forbidden desires; it seeks, serves and fears
God in its inmost soul; it clothes the naked; it
feeds the hungry; it comforts the sorrowful; it
shelters the destitute; it aids and consoles the
sad; it does good to those who do it harm; it
serves those that harm it; it prays for those who
persecute it; it teaches, admonishes and judges
us with the Word of the Lord; it seeks those
who are lost; it binds up what is wounded; it
heals the sick; it saves what is strong; it becomes
all things to all people. The persecution,
suffering and anguish that come to it for the
sake of the Lord's truth have become a glorious
joy and comfort to it.[9]

Weird.

THE PENTECOSTALS (TWENTIETH CENTURY)

Pentecostalism is the most outwardly weird of the movements we're exploring. The Hiberno-Scots were weird
because of their outlandish missionary bravery, the
Cistercians for their asceticism, and the Anabaptists for

their nonconformism. But the Pentecostals were weird just to look at. I mean, speaking in tongues, gyrating and dancing in the Spirit, prophesying and praising—that definitely made them stand out.

There's some debate about whether Pentecostalism got started in Topeka, Kansas, in 1901 or in an Azusa Street mission in Los Angeles in 1906. Some scholars think they can trace the movement's roots back into the late 1800s. Either way, by the very early 1900s, a boisterous new movement was exploding across the USA and eventually around the world. *Life* magazine listed the birth of Pentecostalism as one of the top 100 events of the second millennium. It would have to be considered the most important change in Christianity in the 1900s.

The Topeka evangelist, Charles Parham, and the Azusa Street missioner, William Seymour, both agreed that all the gifts of the Holy Spirit mentioned in the New Testament—including speaking in tongues (*glossolalia*)—are for all Christians today. It's not like no one had spoken in tongues before then, but it had been thought of as a "second blessing," a confirming, devotional experience given to contrite believers. Parham began teaching that speaking in tongues was the initial physical evidence of the infilling of the Holy Spirit. In other words, every Spirit-filled believer should speak in tongues.

But there was more to Pentecostalism than tongues-speaking. Today, the movement is often associated with a flamboyant kind of health-and-wealth preaching pitched at upwardly mobile folks. But in the beginning, in California, it was a working-class movement. It not only attracted the poor and marginalized, but its leaders developed an early theology of poverty, a belief that God had a preference for the poor. As the movement boomed, early Pentecostals interpreted their growth as an example of God's special favor on the poor. This special favor on the poor is a far cry from the prosperity gospel of many late twentieth-century Pentecostals.

Furthermore, Pentecostals were known for their commitments to both racial reconciliation and women's rights. William Seymour, the leader of the Azusa Street Revival, was black; and a woman, Aimee Semple McPherson, was one of Pentecostalism's most famous early leaders. During a still heavily segregated era, many early Pentecostal churches were noted for having blacks and whites, and men and women, worshiping and sharing leadership in the church.

Even less known was that many early Pentecostals were pacifists. Less than a decade after the beginning of their movement, many prominent Pentecostal leaders opposed America's involvement in the outbreak of World War I, and subsequently, every major Pentecostal denomination went on to formally affirm pacifism.

Racially integrated, affirming of women, opposed

to war, on the side of the poor, filled with the Spirit—no one had seen a movement quite like this before. And understandably, they were rebuffed by the other Protestant denominations. Aimee Semple McPherson attracted the most vehement attacks from both secular and church voices. Writer and social commentator Louis Adamic visited McPherson's burgeoning congregation at Angelus Temple and observed how she attracted the poor and disaffected, those who had been drawn to Los Angeles with the promise of new opportunity but whose dreams had been dashed. He described them cruelly as "the drudges of the farms and small-town homes, victims of cruel circumstances, victims of life, slaves of their biological deficiencies. They are diseased, neurotic, unattractive, sexually and intellectually starved, warped and repressed."[10]

Journalist H. L. Mencken agreed. Los Angeles, he opined, "has more morons in it than the whole state of Mississippi, and thousands of them have nothing to do save gape at the movie dignitaries and go to revivals. Aimee . . . piped a tune that struck their fancy."[11]

But it wasn't just nonchurchgoers like Mencken and Adamic who mocked her. Her fellow clergy rejected the weird new movement bubbling away in California. In 1924, Rev. Robert Shuler of Los Angeles' Trinity Methodist Church preached a series of sermons on "McPhersonism," in which he declared, "Cold facts gleaned from extensive investigation and first-hand knowledge of this movement" reveal that McPherson was "neither honest nor genuine." Although "as winsome and attractive as any woman I have ever known," Shuler concluded, she used "hypnotic powers" and "every chord of emotionalism" to sell her "disastrous" theology to unsuspecting temple members.[12]

Despite Shuler's critical view of "McPhersonism," much later even he was forced to admit that while cathedrals and churches across Los Angeles were closing their doors, crowds continued to stream into Angelus Temple.

Like the Celts, the Cistercians, and the Anabaptists before them, the Pentecostals were capable of and committed to a decidedly countercultural form of holiness. They banned alcohol, tobacco, and moviegoing. At various times, some Pentecostal churches frowned on chewing gum, lipstick, short-sleeved dresses, certain soft drinks, and even neckties. Sure, it looked like legalism, but some weirdness is just plain weird, less motivated by the discipline of being different (serving to nurture a culture of eccentricity) than by reactionary responses to the majority culture of the time. As noted, many of their members were drawn from the working class, and a great number were from less reputable backgrounds, where gambling and drinking were corrosive and debilitating practices. The Pentecostals ran soup kitchens and homeless shelters and other charitable initiatives designed to help the less fortunate. But they also fostered a kind of spirituality in which addicts and the indigent could be healed of their afflictions and straighten up and fly right. They endeavored to create communities that were free of the vices they were preaching against. Although I'm not sure why they had a problem with neckties.

GOD REGULARLY BRINGS THE WEIRD BACK

In the first chapter, I referred to weird Christians from throughout history, people like St. Boniface, Anne Hutchinson, John Brown, and Arthur Blessitt. They were eccentrics in the truest sense of the term. But as we've seen, throughout the history of the church, God has raised up strange new movements to stand in contradistinction to the staid or culturally acceptable forms of Christianity of the day. Even though our slow and inexorable drift seems always to be toward conformity, God regularly brings the weird back into our midst. We should look for it, foster it, promote it, join it. Because when God raises up people to help keep Christianity weird, we are reminded again how strange and odd our faith is in the first place. As A. W. Tozer puts it,

A real Christian is an odd number, anyway. He feels supreme love for One whom he has never seen, talks familiarly every day to Someone he cannot see, expects to go to heaven on the virtue of Another, empties himself in order to be full, admits he is wrong so he can be declared right, goes down in order to get up, is strongest when he is weakest, richest when he is poorest and happiest when he feels the worst. He dies so he can live, forsakes in order to have, gives away so he can keep, sees the invisible, hears the inaudible and knows that which passeth knowledge.[13]

But be warned, the Cistercians, the Anabaptists, and the Pentecostals were all viewed suspiciously by the staid and culturally acceptable church of their time, and in the Anabaptists' case, persecuted outright. Similarly, as we saw in the first chapter, the Jesus freaks at Chuck Smith's Calvary Chapel were regarded with some misgiving by the mainstream churches. Any call to keep Christianity weird shouldn't be heard as an encouragement to be hip or popular. None of these weird movements were ever popular ones among the cultural elite. They were devout. They were disciplined. And they turned their worlds upside down.

FOR YOUR CONSIDERATION

1. Can you think of other historical examples, aside from the Celts, Cistercians, Anabaptists, and

Pentecostals, where God raised up weird movements to challenge the conventionality of the mainstream church?

2. What has been your experience of being discipled, or shaped, as a Christian? How does it compare to these historical examples?

3. Which of these historical examples of weird Christians is most intimidating to you? Why? Which is most appealing to you? Why?

4. What's the difference between having your beliefs and behavior shaped by your faith and having your faith shape the way you see the world?

WHAT KILLS THE WEIRD?

*Conformity is the jailer of freedom
and the enemy of growth.*
JOHN F. KENNEDY

Why has Christianity largely become, as Richard Rohr says, "a confirmation of the status quo and business as usual"?[1] Why is it a battle to keep Christianity weird? It appears there are social and religious forces that work against us engaging in deconstructing the "normal" and embracing a dynamic new alternative. Why is it so seductive to be conformed to the patterns of this world?

Most Christians are familiar with Paul's words in Romans 12:2: "Do not conform to the pattern of this world, but be transformed by the renewing of your mind. Then you will be able to test and approve what God's will is—his good, pleasing and perfect will."

When the world around us insists we be normal and

behave like everyone else, what countermands those signals toward normality? Paul insists that the *mind* is the battlefield in the fight to resist being shaped by the values of the society around us. God demands the renewal of our mind.

Elsewhere, Paul says, "You must no longer walk as the Gentiles do, in the futility of their minds. They are darkened in their understanding, alienated from the life of God because of the ignorance that is in them, due to their hardness of heart" (Ephesians 4:17-18, ESV). He goes on to refer to these passions as "deceitful desires" (Ephesians 4:22).

And this isn't just Paul's idea. Peter also tells us we have a mind problem in 1 Peter 1:13-14 (ESV): "Prepar[e] your minds for action. . . . Do not be conformed to the passions of your former ignorance."

In other words, when you were ignorant of the things of God, your passions ran roughshod over your life. You thought you were free, but you were actually enslaved to those passions. You thought you were being wild, but in fact you were behaving exactly like everybody else.

Without the renewal of our minds, we have no control over these desires for conformity and normality. But when Paul commends the renewing of our minds, he's talking about more than clear thinking and logic. We all know that people can be enslaved to all kinds of passions and pleasures, even though they know full well how damaging those things might be. I want to talk about the sanctifying work of the Holy Spirit in renewing our minds a little later, but firstly, let us look at how little power our unrenewed minds have over our core passions.

THE GRANNY SHOT

I was intrigued recently listening to a podcast by Malcolm Gladwell discussing Wilt Chamberlain and his poor free throw shooting.[2] Wilt Chamberlain is known as one of the greatest players in NBA history, but is also renowned as one of the worst free throw shooters to ever play the game. In fact, he was so bad at free throws that opposition players knew that if they fouled him as he headed toward the hoop, he was far less likely to make the free throw than he was to score in open play.

Gladwell compares Wilt Chamberlain with Rick Barry, one of the best free-throw shooters of all time, and a contemporary of Chamberlain's. Barry's technique for free-throw shooting was to throw the ball upward from between his legs, commonly known as the "granny shot." Barry insists that the underarm shot is the more natural, and therefore the more successful way to take free throws. And he has the record to prove it.

In the podcast, Gladwell recounts how Wilt Chamberlain, badly handicapped by his free throw technique, decided to try the granny shot. And it changed everything. His averages for free throws went up dramatically. You'd think this was the end of the story, but it wasn't. Because of the stigma attached to the underarm shooting style, Chamberlain stopped using it the very next season.

Think about that. The greatest player of his era— and one of the greatest of all time—knowing that a certain technique would improve his game, willingly drops it because people would laugh at him. Its very name, suggesting it's the way an old woman would throw, tells us about that stigma (with all due respect to grandmothers who play basketball).

Gladwell, in his inimitably curious style, started asking, *What's the difference between Chamberlain and Barry?* And the answer's not just the seven inches in height between them.

Mark Granovetter, the creator of the threshold model of collective behavior, suggests that people's behavior is shaped by the number of other people already engaging in that particular behavior. All people have their own "threshold," that is, the minimum number of others who must choose a certain behavior before they will. Your threshold is the number of people who have to do something before you join in. And your threshold is determined by a bunch of different factors—social economic status, education, age, personality, and so forth. Also, your threshold is situation specific. You'll calculate the cost and benefit derived from undertaking a certain action in a certain situation and choose to behave accordingly.

Gladwell explains the threshold model by referring to destructive behavior during protests or riots:

> Before Granovetter came along, sociologists tried to explain that kind of puzzling behavior in terms of beliefs. So the thinking went, "You and I have a set of beliefs, but when you throw the rock through the window, something powerful must've happened in the moment to change your beliefs. Something about the crowd transforms the way you think."[3]

Granovetter didn't buy that. Neither does it explain the Chamberlain–Barry conundrum. Chamberlain's *beliefs* told him the underarm shot was a more successful way to shoot free throws. His *behavior*—continuing to shoot free throws overhanded—was in *defiance* of his beliefs. Chamberlain once wrote, "I felt silly, like a sissy, shooting underhanded. I know I was wrong. I know some of the best foul shooters in history shot that way. . . . I just couldn't do it."[4] Logic didn't prevail.

Something else was working on him to make him abandon the technique. Gladwell explains:

> Chamberlain had every incentive in the world
> to keep shooting free throws underhanded and
> he didn't. I think we understand cases where
> people don't do what they ought to do because
> of ignorance. This is not that, this is doing
> something dumb, even though you are fully
> aware that you're doing something dumb.[5]

Granovetter, as summarized by Gladwell, blames Chamberlain's high threshold of collective behavior.

> Thresholds and beliefs sometimes overlap,
> but a lot of the time, they don't. When your
> teenage son is driving 100 miles an hour at
> midnight with three of his friends, it's not
> because he believes that driving 100 miles per
> hour is a good idea. In that moment, his beliefs
> are irrelevant. His behavior is guided by his
> threshold. . . .
>   Everyone's threshold is different. There
> are plenty of radicals and troublemakers
> who might need only slight encouragement
> to throw that rock. Their threshold is
> really low.

But think about your grandmother. She might well need her sister, her grandchildren, her neighbors, her friends from church, all of them to be throwing rocks before she would even dream of joining in. She's got a high threshold.[6]

All that to say, Wilt Chamberlain wouldn't take free throws underarm even though he knew it was better for him because hardly anyone used the granny shot. He had a high threshold of collective behavior. But Rick Barry had a low threshold of behavior. He didn't care that no one was using it. It worked, so he used it. And very successfully.

Have you seen one of those YouTube clips where some guy starts dancing alone, say in a park, and one by one everyone else joins in? That guy has a very low threshold of behavior. He's able to dance carelessly in a park even if he's the only one doing it. And the first person to join him also has a low threshold. But the fiftieth person to join in has a very high threshold. That person had to wait until forty-nine people were already dancing before they'd get on their feet.

Returning to Paul's words about being conformed to the world in Romans 12, you could say that the "deceitful desires" that force us to conform to the world around us are a form of heightened thresholds.

Remember, your threshold is the number of people who have to do something before you join in. Those with high thresholds won't change their behavior unless everyone else does.

How do we countermand those social forces that shape us according to the norm? It's not enough to simply be better informed. That didn't work for Wilt Chamberlain. We need our threshold to be lowered.

So does Christianity heighten our threshold of collective behavior or help lower it? Christianity runs through the filter of expectations we've developed for ourselves in a consumeristic, materialistic, privileged, and enlightened society heightens it. It pushes us toward conventionality and sameness. But the Holy Spirit is in the business of lowering our threshold and making us more daring and less concerned about the judgments of others. This is, in part, what I think Paul is referring to with his expression "the renewal of the mind."

IT'S ALL IN THE MIND

Earlier we looked at Shelly Carson's research into eccentricity. Remember, it was her view that creative, eccentric people are less likely to ignore information that is irrelevant to whatever they're working on. Most people inhibit or filter irrelevant information when we're concentrating on a particular task. But creative people let it all come flooding in.

Similarly, we usually consider people who have a low threshold of collective behavior—like underarm free-throw shooter Rick Barry, or the lone dancer in that YouTube clip—to be eccentric characters. And as we ask whether it's possible to learn to adopt a lower threshold, it will be worth asking a question we began this book with: Can you learn to be creative or eccentric? Or are you born that way?

In other words, can you *become* weird if you're not weird now?

Sadly, most of the research suggests that eccentricity isn't simply learned behavior. It's connected with brain function. Most subjects who exhibit eccentricity or creativity also exhibit signs of something called schizotypal personality.

That sounds scary, I know. But schizotypal people are often very high functioning, talented, and intelligent. They dress outlandishly; they often have strange ways of speaking, usually being quite socially inept; they can be uncomfortable with human intimacy; they can have odd emotional responses to things; they tend to get into supernatural phenomena. In brief, they're impressive, but weird. Schizotypal personality can appear in a variety of forms, including:

- magical thinking (crazy ideas or paranormal beliefs);
- unusual perceptual experiences;
- social anhedonia (a preference for solitary activities); and
- mild paranoia (unfounded feelings that people or objects in the environment may pose a threat).

Gladwell's interview with Rick Barry reveals him to be a loner, hard to get along with, unpopular with teammates, and if not paranoid, certainly under the impression that the world poses challenges he has to defeat. I'm not a psychologist, so I'm not diagnosing Barry as having a schizotypal personality, but he doesn't sound entirely out of the frame.

Since the 1960s, a rash of studies has shown that schizotypal personalities are probably inherited. Way back in 1966, American behavioral geneticist Leonard Heston examined children adopted away from their schizophrenic biological mothers at birth, and found that they were more likely to pursue creative careers and interests than children adopted away from non-afflicted mothers. And the reverse has also proven true. Kids born to non-afflicted biological mothers but raised by schizophrenic parents are less likely to exhibit eccentricity. Multiple studies since then have only confirmed this hypothesis. It seems the combination of creativity and schizotypy tends to run in families. It all points to a genetic component.

So, if you're not weird now, you are not likely to become weirder just by trying harder at it. Ask Wilt Chamberlain.

But don't be discouraged. While your capacity for creativity and eccentricity might be low, and your threshold for collective behavior might be high, there is hope. And it's all in the mind.

RENEWING THE MIND

The renewal of your mind is more than the appropriation of more information about certain matters. And it's more than the abandonment of certain social inhibitions. It is a supernatural work that can only be done by the Holy Spirit.

When Paul says in Romans 12:2, "Be transformed by the *renewing* of your mind" (italics added), he uses a Greek term only rarely found in the New Testament. It appears only two other times in the Bible. One of those usages was also by Paul, where he says in Titus 3:5, "[God] saved us, not because of righteous things we had done, but because of his mercy. He saved us through the washing of rebirth and *renewal* by the Holy Spirit" (italics added). Being saved by God involves this curious combination of washing and renewal. But then it makes sense when we consider Jesus' words to Nicodemus in John 3:5: "Very truly I tell you, no one can enter the kingdom of God unless they are born of water and the Spirit."

Conversion or salvation is accepted as a free gift from God and experienced as both outward washing and inward renewal. Compare Jesus' and Paul's words in this beautiful passage in Ezekiel:

> I will sprinkle clean water on you, and you
> will be clean; I will cleanse you from all your
> impurities and from all your idols. I will give
> you a new heart and put a new spirit in you;
> I will remove from you your heart of stone
> and give you a heart of flesh. And I will put
> my Spirit in you and move you to follow my
> decrees and be careful to keep my laws.
>
> EZEKIEL 36:25-27

Clearly, Jesus fulfils this prophesy from Ezekiel. It is only through Jesus we can be washed clean and given a new spirit. What Paul does in Romans 12 is take this idea of renewal or regeneration by the Holy Spirit and apply it to our minds. According to Paul, the Spirit renews the mind.

And, as Ezekiel says, the Spirit will enable us "to follow my decrees and be careful to keep my laws."

Paul echoes this belief in Titus 3. After referring to the renewal by the Holy Spirit, he goes on to say, "This is a trustworthy saying. And I want you to stress these things, so that those who have trusted in God may be careful to devote themselves to doing what is good" (Titus 3:8).

Remember, in Paul's understanding, doing what is good wasn't the same as doing what is conventional. Doing good, according to Paul, involved bizarre behavior (for the time), like temperance, respect, self-control, loyalty, love, honesty, and trustworthiness (see the full list in Titus 2). This was a time when drunkenness, misogyny, theft, disrespect, dishonesty, and worse was the norm. The only way the earliest Christians could avoid conforming to the patterns of their world—where men treated women as property, where masters mistreated slaves, where slaves stole from masters, where drunkenness and debauchery were commonplace— was to submit to the renewal of their minds by the Holy Spirit.

How does the Spirit do this? It's a mystery, really. When Nicodemus expressed surprise and confusion about Jesus' insistence that he must be born again, Jesus admitted he was speaking of "heavenly things" beyond the Pharisee's ability to understand.

But there are clues to the effect this renewal of the mind will have. Here are a few:

Your eyes will be opened to the light

The Holy Spirit renews our minds by opening our eyes to the truth about Christ's identity. Nicodemus was genuinely lost when Jesus spoke of being born again, and many of his fellow Pharisees were utterly blind to the nature of Jesus' real identity. That's because, as Paul says in 2 Corinthians 4:4, "The god of this age [Satan] has blinded the minds of unbelievers, so that they cannot see the light of the gospel that displays the glory of Christ, who is the image of God."

Renewing our minds involves being exposed to the truth about Jesus. But more than that, it requires our eyes to be opened to that truth by the Spirit. Many people read the Gospels and see them as ancient writings about a long-dead religious leader. But to have one's eyes opened to see the true light of Christ as revealed in Scripture, well, that's the Spirit's work in our lives. Seeing and understanding who Jesus really is, Paul says, will renew your mind and change your life.

You will adopt the posture of humility and worship

When the Spirit renews our minds, all of life becomes an act of worship. That's because the Spirit not only opens our eyes to see who Christ really is but also breaks our hearts to see who we really are. And rather than this being some deathly experience of unending humiliation, seeing ourselves as broken and in need of a savior actually liberates us. It frees us from self-aggrandizement and throws us on the mercy of God with gratitude and love. And when that happens, we find within ourselves there's this growing and nurturing sense of the greatness of God and the beauty of God's love. We see that love being offered to us in myriad ways, and not only through overtly religious means. All of life becomes charged with the presence of God, and we find ourselves wanting to offer more and more of our lives to God as an act of sacrificial worship.

You see, this takes us back to what Paul was saying about the renewal of our minds in Romans 12. When he insists we offer ourselves as living sacrifices—each of us submitting our whole life as an act of worship—he says we should do so "in view of God's mercy" (Romans 12:1). The Spirit reveals that mercy to us and transforms us into worshipers.

You will become more like Jesus

When the Spirit renews our minds by revealing Christ's identity and breaking our hearts to evoke humility and worship, then and only then are we ready to be reshaped into the likeness of Christ. In 2 Corinthians 3:18, Paul says, "And we all, who with unveiled faces contemplate the Lord's glory, are being transformed into his image with ever-increasing glory, which comes from the Lord, who is the Spirit." The Holy Spirit renews our minds as we contemplate or behold the glory of the Lord. As we steadfastly focus on Jesus, devoting ourselves as his students or disciples, the Spirit renews our thinking and our behavior, and we become more like him. He actually transforms us into the image of the Son of God. The Holy Spirit makes us weird like Jesus was weird.

LOWERING YOUR THRESHOLD

To return to Mark Granovetter's work on thresholds of collective behavior, what can transform ordinary, conventional people, shaped by the values of this world, into radical disciples of Jesus? What can take churchgoers with high thresholds of collective behavior and lower their threshold so they will stand out from the crowd and make a difference for Christ? If a person's capacity for creativity or eccentricity is already set according to their schizotypal DNA, there's got to be something that can help ordinary people like you and me become more weird. Surely, it's only the renewal of the mind by the Holy Spirit.

An encounter with the Spirit and the ongoing process of yielding oneself to the process of sanctification are the only things that can countermand your natural impulse to be normal. This is because the Spirit's work is to open our eyes, to break our pride, and to make us more like Jesus. And Jesus was weird.

Consider Amanda Berry Smith, the most famous evangelist you've probably never heard of.

Born into slavery in 1837, married at 17, widowed at 26, by the time Smith was 32 she had lost her second husband and four of her five children had died in abject poverty. When one son died in her arms because she couldn't afford medical treatment, she was struck by the awful thought that she also had no money to bury him.

Barely educated, and eking out a miserable existence in Philadelphia, Smith learned how to be invisible in mixed company, as many African American women were required to do, even in free states like Pennsylvania.

"I always tried to avoid anything like pushing myself, or going where I was not wanted," she explained in her autobiography.[7]

Painfully shy, and intimidated around white people, you could say Amanda Berry Smith had a very high threshold of collective behavior. She did anything not to stand out. She dressed like a "pious Mammie" (in her words), always wearing a plain poke bonnet and a brown or black Quaker wrap, and she bowed and scraped and appeared nervous in public. She found employment doing menial domestic jobs like mending clothes or washing dishes.

And that might have been all we ever knew about

Amanda Berry Smith except for one night in September 1868. She encountered the Holy Spirit that night and was never the same again. She described the experience this way:

> A wave came over me, and such a welling up
> in my heart. . . . How I have lived through it
> I cannot tell, but the blessedness of the love
> and the peace and power I can never describe.
> O, what glory filled my soul! The great vacuum
> in my soul began to fill up; it was like a pleasant
> draught of cool water, and I felt it. I wanted to
> shout Glory to Jesus! . . . Just as I put my foot
> on the top step I seemed to feel a hand, the
> touch of which I cannot describe. It seemed to
> press me gently on the top of my head, and I felt
> something part and roll down and cover me like
> a great cloak! I felt it distinctly; it was done in a
> moment, and O what a mighty peace and power
> took possession of me![8]

She immersed herself in the African Methodist Episcopal Church and soon found herself singing and preaching at revival meetings and church services.

In 1878, Smith arranged for her only surviving daughter, Mazie, to study in England and the two set sail for Plymouth. They were the only African Americans on the ship. When the captain heard she had done some preaching with the African Methodist Episcopal Church, and conscious that he had no other ministers on board, he asked Smith to conduct services. She'd never spoken in public to white people before. And the white passengers had never heard a black woman preach before! The response was remarkable. So impressed were the passengers on board that when they disembarked in England, word soon spread that a great evangelist had landed on their shores.

Amanda Smith was considered an exotic creature by British congregations. Most people had not only never heard a black female preacher, they'd never heard *of* one. That she was a former slave only added to the novelty. The shy, retiring washerwoman became something of a celebrity.

This led to a two-year stint preaching and singing in the UK. From there, Amanda Smith traveled to India as an evangelist and then on to Africa, where she spent eight years in Liberia and West Africa conducting revival meetings and establishing orphanages. When she returned to the US in 1890, no one who knew her as a young impoverished widow and ex-slave would have recognized the world-traveling evangelist and preacher before them.

In her later years, she continued to travel the world, preaching and overseeing the establishment of the imposingly named Amanda Smith Orphanage and Industrial Home for Abandoned and Destitute Colored Children in Chicago.

Amanda Smith had been transformed by the renewal of her mind, and she was never the same.

I began this chapter with a question: What kills the weird? What stops us from stepping out or standing up? What raises our threshold of collective behavior and keeps us in normality? For Amanda Smith, it was fear, intimidation, racism, poverty, insecurity. As an ex-slave and an impoverished washerwoman, she was shamed into silence and anonymity. This was the same shame that stopped Wilt Chamberlain from taking underarm free throws.

What else could break those bonds but for the work of the Spirit? After her encounter with the Holy Spirit that night in 1878, Amanda Smith announced dramatically, "But I belong to Royalty, and am well acquainted with the King of Kings, and am better known and better understood among the great family above than I am on earth."[9] There was no stopping her after that.

FOR YOUR CONSIDERATION

1. How would you rate your threshold of collective behavior? Is it low or high?

2. How would you rate your level of cognitive disinhibition? Low or high?

3. What people, groups, or communities do you have around you to help you and nurture you as you seek to be more different for Christ's sake?

4. When you consider Paul's encouragement to be "transformed by the renewal of your mind," how do you think your life would be changed if you truly took these words to heart? When was the last time you prayed to be transformed by the renewal of your mind?

SEEING THINGS WEIRDLY

*There are two ways of seeing: with the body
and with the soul. The body's sight can sometimes
forget, but the soul remembers forever.*

ALEXANDRE DUMAS

Back in chapter 3, we looked at the weirdness of Jesus, particularly in relation to his views on the religious leaders of Israel. You'll remember he was quite scathing in his criticism of the Pharisees for their attempts to hem the reign of God within the borders of Israel. He referred to himself as the Good Shepherd who had come to lead his sheep to freedom and to call sheep from other pens to join them in this magnificent, multiracial, international community of redeemed ones. This community would be born "from above," not inheriting their membership at their earthly birth.

But as we saw in the previous chapter, the freedom to which Jesus leads his community is not some free-for-all society of carefree abandon. It is a disciplined community whose righteousness exceeds that of Pharisees while barely resembling it at all. As the earliest Christians discovered, through teaching and worship and the fostering of a new set of habits, they were being recreated by Jesus to live out the values of his Kingdom while still functioning in the social and political landscape of the Roman Empire. Jesus referred to this as being like salt and light in the world.

These metaphors, like the sheep and shepherd metaphors we looked at earlier, are so familiar to Christians today that their original potency is somewhat diminished. But describing his followers as being like salt and light is incredibly evocative. Here's how he puts it:

> You are the salt of the earth. But if the salt loses its saltiness, how can it be made salty again? It is no longer good for anything, except to be thrown out and trampled underfoot.
>
> You are the light of the world. A town built on a hill cannot be hidden. Neither do people light a lamp and put it under a bowl. Instead they put it on its stand, and it gives light to everyone in the house. In the same way, let your light shine before others, that they may see your good deeds and glorify your Father in heaven.
>
> MATTHEW 5:13-16

Salt added to a stew flavors every spoonful of the meal. Likewise, this new, multiracial, international society of redeemed ones, called by Christ, will permeate every aspect of the empire, changing its very tone and tenor. The church should flavor the empire in which it finds itself. Likewise, Jesus' reference to a well-lit city on a hill or a lamp on a lampstand illustrates the same idea. You can't contain the light. Once a lamp is lit, the light permeates every part of the room. It's pervasive.

Jesus calls his followers to infiltrate every aspect of the empire, to bring flavor and light to its darkest and most tasteless corners, something the Pharisees were loath to do. They were terrified of offending the empire and had developed a form of Judaism that would have seemed inconsequential and provincial to the Roman authorities—chiefly, Sabbath-keeping, tithing, and Temple worship. Jesus was having none of that. He openly flouted their conventions and dismissed them for their fear and hypocrisy, for emphasizing the letter of the law over its spirit, and for their greed and self-righteousness. And all the while he was gathering a people to himself, a strange society unlike anything the world had ever seen.

Reflecting on this passage in his commentary on Matthew's Gospel, theologian Stanley Hauerwas identifies several hallmarks of the new society Jesus was forming—it was voluntary, it was integrated, and it was countercultural.[1]

1. *Jesus' new order is a voluntary society.* As we've noted, you couldn't be born into this new order via a fleshly birth, as the Pharisees had assumed. You had to be born again, or born "from above." Jesus, the one who came from above, as it were, invites all people, including Gentiles, to repent of their sin and acknowledge him as their King. This includes renouncing your former citizenship. As the Anabaptists discovered 1,500 years later, Jesus demands your sole allegiance.

2. *Jesus' new order is an integrated society.* If Gentiles can gain access to Jesus' new society, it is clear he intended it to welcome all comers. We see that very early in the church's history with the baptism of Gentiles like the Ethiopian eunuch (Acts 8:26-38) and the household of Cornelius (Acts 10:1-48). Hauerwas describes the church this way: "It was mixed racially, with both Jews and Gentiles; mixed religiously, with fanatical keepers of the law and advocates of liberty from all forms; with both radical monotheists and others just in the process of disentangling their minds from idolatry; mixed economically with members both rich and poor."[2]

3. *Jesus' new order is a countercultural society.* I can't explain this better than Hauerwas does:

> When he called his society together
> Jesus gave its members a new way of
> life to live. He gave them a new way to
> deal with offenders—by forgiving them.
> He gave them a new way to deal with
> violence—by suffering. He gave them
> a new way to deal with money—by
> sharing it. He gave them a new way to
> deal with problems of leadership—by
> drawing upon the gift of every member,
> even the most humble. He gave them a
> new way to deal with a corrupt society—
> by building a new order, not smashing
> the old. He gave them a new pattern of
> relationship between man and woman,
> between parent and child, between
> master and slave, in which was made
> concrete a radical new vision of what it
> means to be a human person. He gave
> them a new attitude toward the state
> and toward the "enemy nation."[3]

This "new way of life to live" is the way of the weird. It's a completely alternate way of life from everyone else in the world. As we've seen, it requires a complete renewal of the mind by the Holy Spirit to achieve such a lifestyle. And it involves a new set of lived habits to reinforce these values and sustain them in your everyday life. It takes all the discipline of the Celts or the Cistercians. As a result, weird followers of Jesus will see the world entirely differently. They'll see things weirdly.

In the end, our faith is not just about a set of practices or shared beliefs, important though they are. Primarily, it is a new way of seeing. All our learning and newly acquired habits provide the scaffolding, but at the center, a newly sighted person is emerging. I think this is what the writer of the letter to the Hebrews is getting at when he writes, "Now faith is confidence in what we hope for and assurance about what we do not see" (Hebrews 11:1). Older translations use the better-known phrase "the evidence of things not seen," which I take to mean belief in things you cannot prove. Followers of Jesus see things—and believe things—they cannot prove. To put it in a nonsensical way, *they see things they cannot see.* That's faith.

Jewish writer Harold Kushner agrees,

> True religion goes beyond making sense. It does not offend reason, it transcends reason. People do not start to see the world differently because someone has written a book giving them good

reasons for doing so. They do it because they feel they have been touched by the presence of God.[4]

Let us examine how this new way of seeing things weirdly works itself out in our world today.

WHEN TEMPTED TO CHOOSE SIDES, LOOK INSIDE

In a recent *New York Times* piece, Emily Badger and Niraj Chokshi revealed the following curious fact:

> In 1960, just 5 percent of Republicans and 4 percent of Democrats said they would be unhappy if a son or daughter married someone from the other party. In a YouGov survey from 2008 . . . 27 percent of Republicans and 20 percent of Democrats said they'd be "somewhat" or "very upset" by that prospect. By 2010, that share had jumped to half of Republicans and a third of Democrats.[5]

Get ready for a remake of the Sidney Poitier classic *Guess Who's Coming to Dinner*, in which a kindly and patrician couple of Republicans are shocked to discover their daughter is engaged to a (gulp) Bernie Sanders supporter. (Or a Democrat couple meeting their daughter's fiancé in his "Make America Great Again" hat).

But seriously, what is going on??

By most people's reckoning, the 2016 presidential campaign was one of the most divisive in American history. The vitriol and animosity expressed by supporters of one candidate toward supporters of another was astonishing. Even those of us who are nonpartisan and who refused to support any particular candidate found ourselves abused on social media if we posted anything critical of a candidate. And I mean *any* candidate.

But according to Badger and Chokshi, this gulf of fury and self-righteousness wasn't a new thing in 2016. It had been building for many years.

Back in 2008, Bill Bishop wrote *The Big Sort: Why the Clustering of Like-Minded America Is Tearing Us Apart* in an attempt to understand the deep fault lines developing across American society. Americans weren't just being sorted into red or blue states. Society was being sorted into black/white/Latino/Asian categories. Americans were finding themselves categorized as liberals or conservatives, as boomers or Gen Xers, as Protestant or Catholic, as mainline or evangelical, and the list goes on.

Bishop wrote, "As people seek out the social settings they prefer—as they choose the group that makes them feel the most comfortable—the nation grows more politically segregated—and the benefit that ought to come with having a variety of opinions is lost to the righteousness that is the special entitlement of homogeneous groups."[6]

Add to this: Each group lives in its own echo chamber, with its own preferred TV news networks, talkback hosts, newspaper columnists, social commentators, blog writers, conventions, and so forth.

Bishop continues,

> Like-minded, homogeneous groups squelch dissent, grow more extreme in their thinking, and ignore evidence that their positions are wrong. As a result, we now live in a giant feedback loop, hearing our own thoughts about what's right and wrong bounced back to us by the television shows we watch, the newspapers and books we read, the blogs we visit online, the sermons we hear, and the neighborhoods we live in.[7]

Badger and Chokshi confirm this. Quoting Pew Research, they found that 68 percent of Republicans and 62 percent of Democrats say they identify with their political party primarily out of their *opposition* to the other party. Indeed, they found that "45 percent of Republicans and 41 percent of Democrats felt that the other party's policies posed a *threat* to the nation."[8]

They conclude by quoting Shanto Iyengar saying, "We have all of these data which converge on the bottom-line conclusion that [political] party is the No. 1 cleavage in contemporary American society."[9]

That means partisan politics is a more divisive issue than race.

The obvious acrimony of recent political campaigns in Britain and France reveal that this is certainly not exclusively an American problem.

In this overheated environment, it's incredibly tempting to choose a side. And then to hitch our sense of identity and self-esteem to whether that side "wins" or not.

Surely, we know that trying to win some culture war by electing the "right" party to power is folly. What Christian genuinely believes that the two-party political system is ever going to deliver the kind of liberation Jesus promised?

In fact, Christians should have very little confidence in the political process at all. And that's not a cynical stance. In saying this, I'm not proposing a complete withdrawal from politics. I'm saying we can't be confident in political processes to deliver the liberation Jesus promised. We know that the goal of the political process can't simply be "liberation" *from* something. We must be liberated *to* something. Otherwise we are liberated only to ourselves and self-expression, which is another form of bondage.

The church is called to offer such a space: a social reality that displays the Kingdom of God as a foretaste of things to come. Weird Christians know there can be no political theology of liberation without ecclesiology, and no liberation without the people of God.

Christians shouldn't be looking around for the next political liberator. We need to be *looking inside* for evidence of spiritual renewal—the renewal of the mind and the living out of a new set of habits and values. As we heard Stanley Hauerwas explain earlier, this means the followers of Jesus are much less concerned with choosing sides or smashing their political enemies and much more committed to building a new order, the Jesus way.

WHEN TEMPTED TO LOOK AROUND, LOOK UP

Weird Cities value things like beer, bikeability, hipsterism, outdoor recreation, the farm-to-table movement, great restaurants, the arts, and alternative lifestyles. The values of Christianity both align with and diverge from these kinds of things. But we need to be less concerned about looking around at others and seeking some kind of relevance by mirroring the world's values, and more concerned with developing a capacity to affirm those values that align with biblical teaching, while effectively challenging the social mores and conventions that differ with biblical piety and compassion.

And in what ways can Christian piety be seen as appealingly weird again?

In 2017, former football coach turned evangelist Dave Daubenmire gained notoriety for his televised call for "a more violent Christianity."[10] Explaining that "the Bible is full of violence," Daubenmire went on to say that "the only thing that is going to save Western civilization is a more aggressive, a more violent Christianity."[11] To illustrate this point, he referred to President Trump's behavior at a NATO summit where he shoved the prime minister of Montenegro aside so that he could stand in front of the group of assembled leaders. Christianity should be like that, Daubenmire explained.

"[President Trump] is large and in charge.

"Look at him," Daubenmire screamed gleefully while watching the clip. "They're all little puppies, ain't nobody barking at him. . . . He's walking in authority. He walked to the front and center and they all know it, too, man. He just spanked them all. . . .

"The Lord is showing us a picture of the authority we should be walking in."

Warming to his subject, Daubenmire then cited Republican congressional candidate Greg Gianforte's vicious assault on a reporter as another example for the church to follow.

> "People are sick and tired of it," he said. "They're saying, 'Yes, a fighter! Go, dude, go!' . . . Who won? The dude that took the other dude to the ground."

Gianforte later apologized for his actions, but Daubenmire still thinks the body-slamming congressman is a great example of the kind of violent Christianity we need.

I'm not going to reflect on the level of commitment to Jesus shared by Donald Trump or Greg Gianforte, but when I'm looking around for examples of what Christlike behavior might look like, I don't think they're at the top of my must-watch list. Indeed, I'm going to suggest we don't even *need* a must-watch list. We need to look up to the example of Jesus and try to figure out what weird, unlikely Christlike behavior should look like. Let me remind you again of Stanley Hauerwas's word:

> [Jesus] gave them a new way to deal with offenders—by forgiving them. He gave them a new way to deal with violence—by suffering. He gave them a new way to deal with money—by sharing it. He gave them a new way to deal with

problems of leadership—by drawing upon the
gift of every member, even the most humble.[12]

In my home of Australia, I have experienced this in a
powerful way through my involvement in a movement
called Love Makes a Way. For many years, the Australian
federal government has enacted a brutal policy of man-
datory detention for all refugees claiming asylum on our
shores. For many asylum seekers, this means repatria-
tion to prisons on remote islands in the Pacific Ocean
as they wait for years for their claim for asylum to be
processed. The living conditions and pervasive absence
of hope there is destroying thousands of lives, particularly those of the children caught up in this horror. In
fact, this cruel and unusual punishment meted out to
men, women, and children is designed to discourage
more refugees from attempting to arrive in the country.
They are punishing children to prosecute their policy of
reducing refugee numbers. It's wrong.

Love Makes a Way is a movement of Christians seeking an end to these inhumane policies through prayer
and nonviolent action. I have participated in several
such actions, the most dramatic being an act of civil dis-
obedience in the office of the prime minister of Australia.
Together with a number of clergy—a Catholic nun, an
Anglican priest, several Uniting Church ministers—
I entered the waiting area of his Sydney office and

kneeled in prayer, ignoring the requests of the staff to leave. Transcripts of the incident reports from the detention centers had just been leaked to the media, detailing sexual assault, suicide attempts, depression, anxiety, the dearth of medical treatment, and more. We quietly read sections of these transcripts aloud and prayed for the men, women, and children involved. We sang hymns and spiritual songs. We wept. I cried as I read aloud a report about a young girl swallowing stones in an attempt to end her life.

The Prime Minister's staff called the police, who arrived to find an elderly nun and an assortment of ministers praying peaceably. They didn't want to arrest us because they knew the media were outside and the story wouldn't play well. They suggested to the office staff that they leave us alone. Surely, they thought, they can't pray for that long.

But after eight hours of ceaseless prayer and worship, the office staff wanted to go home and we were still refusing to leave. The police returned and arrested us. I was taken by the arm by a young officer and escorted from the premises.

"I was here this morning shortly after you arrived," he told me. "Have you been praying that *whole time*?"

He was incredulous. I guess if you're not used to praying, you might wonder how people could do it all day. So I told him, yes, we'd been praying, reading transcripts, and singing spiritual songs all day, without even a toilet break. As we emerged out onto the street where photographers snapped our picture, and while his hand was still gripping my elbow, he asked, "Why?"

In a world where beating up your enemies or pushing and shoving those who get in your way is normal and acceptable, praying earnestly for the defenseless is weird. In a world where you only ever speak up for yourself or your own rights, giving voice to the voiceless is strange. In a world of busyness, hustle, bustle, and social media, kneeling in a circle with brothers and sisters and focusing a whole day on worship and prayer and reflection is utterly bizarre.

"Why?" I responded. "It's a nonviolent action, a public witness to injustice, and a shot at dramatically awakening people's conscience about this issue. We're trying to point to a better way, the way of justice, peace, and love. Because that's what Jesus taught us to do."

We were walking down the street by this time, away from our supporters, toward the police station, when the fresh-faced young cop admitted to me quietly, "I agree with what you're doing."

Would he have been the least bit open to agreeing with what we were doing if we'd employed violence to prosecute our case for change? Looking up involves allowing the disciplines of God's people—prayer, self-sacrifice, generosity, kindness, and humility—to rule the day, to shape our response to the hatred, division, and injustice that wrack our world, as weird as that might seem.

WHEN LOOKING INTO THE FUTURE, LOOK DOWN

Weird Cities are open-minded, friendly, and art-infused. Their once-derelict downtown areas are now teeming with organic food shops, funky galleries, craft breweries, stores for outdoor enthusiasts, and one-of-a-kind boutiques. The culture is laid-back and accepting. We all know these cities aren't perfect. But by entering into the cultural and social rhythms of our cities, Christians can rediscover the yearnings of their neighbors, yearnings that can only be fully satisfied in Christ.

"Looking down" involves a commitment to deep, incarnational living. It includes cultural exegesis and discernment, and the development of highly contextualized models of ministry. And many Christian leaders are letting go of the small story of church growth and embracing the big story of finding out what God is doing in their neighborhood and joining in.

In 2016, Christiana Rice and Tim Soerens from the Parish Collective, a network of place-based church initiatives, developed what they called "the five signs of the Parish Movement."[13] These were descriptors of what life can be like when you're looking down. I will summarize them from their original article:

1. *Centering on Christ*: Place-based communities of faith don't only believe in Christ but also see the Incarnational as the inspiration and shape of their work in the neighborhood.

2. *Inhabiting Our Parish*: Recovering the European Christendom idea of parish as a discrete geographical boundary of influence, place-based churches inhabit their place/parish by joining God's renewal in, with, and for their place. As Rice and Soerens describe it, place-based churches are "learning to accept our limitations as a gift from God, live with intentionality, be known by our actual neighbors and tangibly love those around us. We seek to participate in God's renewal by listening to, serving, and caring for the land and the people where we live, work and play."[14]

3. *Gathering to Remember*: Far from melting into the rhythms of their place to be indistinguishable from any other good neighbor, place-based believers meet together regularly to "remember the larger story of our faith, rehearse the kind of people God desires us to be in the parish, and encourage one another in love and discernment."[15]

In fact, the Parish Collective believes it is all the more crucial to gather together as they are contributing to God's renewal in the parish and as they collaborate with neighbors who don't necessarily share their faith in Christ.

4. *Collaborating for God's Renewal*: When you look down and truly encounter the depths of the problems confronting neighborhoods, it's impossible to believe the church can fix things by themselves. That's the old patronage model of service provision that allowed the church to do a great deal of good throughout history but impeded the church's level of meaningful connection with its neighbors. Place-based churches know they need to collaborate with neighbors from other traditions, faiths, and experiences and believe that doing so doesn't compromise their devotion to Christ.

5. *Linking across Parishes*: This is pretty much what the Parish Collective does. It helps place-based initiatives connect with other Christian communities, both regionally and globally, to learn together and encourage each other in this challenging but rewarding work.

Who could forget the dramatic inferno that engulfed the twenty-four-floor Grenfell Tower in west London in

2017! It started with the sparking of a faulty fridge-freezer in a fourth-floor flat. But the speed with which the fire consumed the 129 apartments was breathtaking. It quickly incinerated the whole building as families appeared at their windows screaming for help. Some people tied bedsheets into a makeshift rope to escape the furnace. Some leaped to the ground below. It was all too horrible.

We know now that over seventy people lost their lives and many others were injured. Hundreds were displaced, escaping the flames with nothing but their lives and the pajamas they had been sleeping in. We also know that the community response to this tragedy was incredible. The outpouring of generosity and kindness was heartwarming. But it began in an interesting way.

At 3:00 a.m. the night of the fire, Rev. Alan Everett, the vicar of the nearby St. Clement's Church of England, was woken by a call from a fellow priest who lived in Grenfell Tower. The priest had called to alert Everett that he had a national disaster unfolding almost literally on his doorstep.

Alan Everett ran to the church and turned the lights on and opened the doors wide. He didn't know what else to do.

Soon people started stumbling out of the dark, making their way to the safety of the church. Passersby and people who'd come to help also found refuge there.

Shortly after sunrise, the members of St. Clement's began serving breakfast to those who had fled the tower and to the weary volunteers. Local restaurants had donated food. Neighbors turned up with clothes and blankets. Soon the church sanctuary resembled a disaster relief station.

The church became a refuge, a triage unit, a feeding station, an aid-delivery center. All because the local vicar simply turned the lights on and opened the door.

And because they were *there*!

There's no doubt that the new churches planted in repurposed warehouses in industrial areas on the edges of towns are full of equally generous people. But often, those churches have no proximity to their cities. Usually, their minister doesn't live near the church building, anyway. If he or she decided to open the church, they would first need to drive across town, by which time the need to house, care for, and assess the injuries of the victims of a fire like the one at Grenfell Tower would have gone elsewhere.

After the blaze, locals harbored considerable resentment toward politicians. They had been informing the authorities that Grenfell Tower was a firetrap, but their calls had gone unheeded. Now that scores of people were dead and hundreds made homeless, the prime minister, the Leader of the Opposition, and the Lord Mayor all turned up for a photo opportunity with the community.

But they weren't fooling anyone. It wasn't the government or the City of London that snapped into action on the night of the fire. It was the church.

St. Clement's is a small, poor church, but the people of the parish trust them. Their local charity provides assistance to thousands of locals every year. But their numbers aren't huge, and they're struggling to keep the lights on and the doors open.

How ironic then, that the simple act of turning the lights on and opening the doors should have had such an extraordinary impact on the night of the Grenfell Tower fire.

As Alan Everett says, "We are called to share in the brokenness and the forgottenness of the people we serve."[16]

Giles Fraser, writing in *The Guardian*, concluded, "This being permanently present is no small thing. Not least because, as Christians believe, the light will always beckon people out of the darkness."[17]

I think there's more to the mission of the church than merely being present. Unexplained acts of kindness and love do not in themselves constitute the full mission of God's people. We need to share Christ, to offer hope, to develop ministries that allow the community to collaborate with us and be served by us. But you don't get to do any of that stuff unless you can embrace this "no small thing" of being permanently present.

One of the central tenets of the church growth movement is that nongrowth is just as important to discover as growth. If the church isn't growing in a given area, a new strategy is needed to move to another, more promising area.

If the Church of England had embraced that strategy, there probably wouldn't have been a St. Clement's for the victims of that fire to take refuge in.

N. T. Wright talks about how, in Christ, heaven has invaded earth, and the whole world is now holy land. The work of God's people is to claim all places as God's and to fashion ways for others to see the holiness, the new creation unfurling around them. On the night of the Grenfell Tower disaster, in the midst of horror and darkness and tragedy, the little, local parish church was holy land. But Wright says the placing of all things under the reign of Jesus involves more than just charitable work:

> The church . . . [should] go straight from worshipping in the sanctuary to debating in the council chamber—discussing matters of town planning, of harmonizing and humanizing beauty in architecture, in green spaces, in road traffic schemes, and . . . in environmental work, creative and healthy farming methods, and proper use of resources. If it is true, as I have

argued, that the whole world is now God's holy land, we must not rest as long as that land is spoiled and defaced. This is not an extra to the church's mission. It is central.[18]

On June 14, 2017, in North Kensington, west London, that involved being permanently present, and turning on the lights, and opening the doors.

What does it look like in your neighborhood?

After Giles Fraser reported on the beautiful work of St. Clement's, a few readers left comments on the Guardian site:

> i am not a religious person but i have to say the local churches & people during this unimaginable horror have gone someway to restore my faith in humanity when the victims have manifestly been failed by the well heeled & well paid that are supposed to look after us in times of crisis.

> I am not a religious person either. But I do envy (the irony of sin) the sense of community that the church/mosque provides.

> Local churches and church people: yes indeed. But 'the Church' ? As irrelevant as ever.[19]

Are we listening?

FOR YOUR CONSIDERATION

1. Where do you feel pressure to choose sides? What helps you to "look inside"? What helps you to resist the pressure?

2. Where do you feel temptation to conform to the culture around you? What helps you to "look up"? What helps you to resist the temptation?

3. When was the last time you "looked down"? What are the needs of your community today? How can you help to address them in a distinctly Christian way?

7

IF WE'RE NOT WEIRD, WE'RE DOING IT WRONG

Not being able to fully understand God is frustrating,
but it is ridiculous for us to think we have
the right to limit God to something we
are capable of comprehending.

FRANCIS CHAN

So far, I have spoken of Christian weirdness in terms of locating our identities off center and putting God at the heart of things. I have also said that should result in the renewing of our minds and the transformation of our values so we look weird or unconventional to those around us. Christians should push back against convention in the church and in the church's witness. We should also develop lifestyle rhythms that help us to continue faithfully improvising in communal and personal discipleship. And we need to take the example of Jesus as our guide. In other words, when in doubt, follow Jesus.

NOT WEIRD LIKE *THAT*

Christianity needs to retain its weirdness, to continue its ancient tradition of being unconventional, surprising, and eccentric in the true sense of the word. But in saying that, I don't want it to be misconstrued as a call for the church to be zany or wacky. I think our world is tiring of stupid stunts and religious mania. And Christians have been more than willing to look like maniacs.

In 2013, the pastor of a 12,000-member church in Ohio attracted a bit of media attention when he zip-lined through the church's auditorium over the heads of his congregation to the strains of the *Mission Impossible* theme and landed behind his pulpit, ready to preach. While many other churches were celebrating the ancient season of Lent, he was launching his *Mission Impossible* sermon series leading into Easter.[1] Cool! At least, I think that's the reaction he wanted.

Ohio must be the place for these in-church publicity stunts, because another pastor from a nearby church rode a wild horse in front of his congregation as a sermon illustration one Sunday. Hoping to attract a few extra attendees to the church, he removed the front few pews and laid down plastic and dirt to create a temporary rodeo arena. He then mounted a wild bucking horse and rode it for ten minutes as part of his sermon entitled "Conquer the Beast."[2]

We can all think of stupid stuff Christians do to attract attention to themselves, all in the name of "sharing Christ."

A Texan pastor spent three days locked in a six-foot plexiglass cube atop his church to attract more members.[3]

Another one, from Georgia, rides his motorcycle through a wall of fire and over a bus, all set up in the church parking lot.[4]

A Texan pastor set up a bed on the roof of his church so he and his wife could encourage the church's week of "congregational copulation" by spending twenty-four hours expressing their love for each other up there.[5]

And in Joplin, Missouri, one church gave away AR-15 rifles as a Father's Day promotion.[6]

Bemoaning these kinds of bizarre schemes, Chicago pastor Seth Tower Hurd recalls his own experience growing up as a young person in a stunt-crazy church,

The "Christian Power Team" came to town
and tore phone books in half, flexed their
comically massive biceps, then threw in an
altar call to commit to Jesus. Every Easter, my
family attended a "Passion Play," depicting
the last hours of Jesus' life on the lawn of the
courthouse, within viewing distance of three of
the county's rowdiest bars. When I was a teen,
one church brought in a female abstinence

rapper (can't make that one up) to spit some sick verses about her lack of a sex life. This "hip-hop outreach," closed out with each high school student receiving a "sex can wait" cloth bracelet.[7]

Sure, that kind of behavior might be termed eccentric, but it's not what I'm talking about when I call on the church to be more weird. Here, we need to distinguish between the kind of countercultural weirdness that evokes curiosity and genuine interest in the way of Jesus, and publicity stunts. As we've seen, the former is really difficult, while the latter is easy. Too easy.

I have a friend who told me about a megachurch in her very well-to-do neighborhood that spent $10,000 buying gas cards at the local gas station and handing them out to neighbors. They also called the local radio and television news stations to be there when the crowds lined up for their free gas. When the radio station started getting callers saying they were in line behind a Mercedes, and when the television news footage showed a Lexus in line as well, my friend had a few questions about how much more good the church could have done with $10,000. She started to wonder whether this was a selfless, costly act of generosity or a shameless grab for attention.

Let's face it, if our neighbors think we're weird because we hold to a totally alternate ethic that includes

pacifism, the costly sharing of our possessions, the practice of radical hospitality, the offer of forgiveness and
grace, the protection of the environment, and a totally
different understanding of family, that's great. If, however, they suspect our motives aren't altruistic and we're
really just drawing attention to ourselves, it would have
been better if we'd stayed silent.

These attention-seeking stunts aren't just silly. They
can be downright dangerous as well. In 2010, a church in
Gainesville, Florida, the Dove World Outreach Center,
announced plans to commemorate the attack on the
Pentagon and the World Trade Center on September 11
by burning copies of the Quran on the church grounds.
You might recall they were talked out of it, with President
Obama even weighing in on the discussion.[8]

This kind of behavior might be considered weird,
but it's easy-weird. And easy-weird doesn't cut it. It's the
church equivalent of the Keep Portland Weird Unipiper.
You know him, the guy in the Darth Vader mask and kilt
who rides a unicycle around Portland while playing "The
Imperial March" from *Star Wars* on his flame-shooting
bagpipes. His actual name is Brian Kidd, and by profes-
sion he's a quantum spatial acquisition manager. In his
spare time, he goofs off as the Unipiper around the streets
of Portland and at sporting events.[9] It's all good, harm-
less fun, but if that was all there was to the Weird Cities
thing, it wouldn't even be worth mentioning.

Church publicity stunts are the religious version of the Unipiper. If there's no seriously deep weirdness going on behind it all, it's just flaming bagpipes.

As we've seen, serious, deep weirdness takes time and discipline. To eschew the values of consumerism, materialism, and militarism so entrenched in our society, we need to undertake the kind of deep discipleship we observed among the Celts and the Cistercians and the other countercultural Christian groups we looked at in chapter 5.

But now I want to introduce a third kind of weirdness we need to embrace.

WEIRD LIKE *THIS*

To recap: First, we're weird because our identity is found in God, not our own egos. Second, we're weird because, in following Christ, we embrace an entirely unconventional ethic at odds with the values of this world. And third, we're weird because we believe some crazy supernatural stuff.

Remember the witches from Shakespeare's *Macbeth*? You know, "Double, double, toil and trouble"? Well, they're only called witches once in that play. Shakespeare refers to them as being "weird" six times. He uses the Old English term *wyrd*, which means fate, and as there's three of them and they're described as sisters, most people think Shakespeare is suggesting they are the three Fates of classical mythology. The Fates were three sister deities who were believed to control when you would be born, how long you would live, and how and when you would die. So to be "wyrd" was to believe in supernatural forces that control destiny and life.

By the nineteenth century, it had become a term to describe something baffling or mystifying, something that couldn't be fully explained. Weird didn't mean unconventional back then so much as otherworldly or supernatural.

We shouldn't forget this aspect of our weirdness. We don't believe in the ancient Greek Fates. We believe God controls life and destiny. But that's still pretty freaky and unearthly. There's a danger that in trying to make our faith sensible and accessible to others, we leech it of its supernatural elements. I think we need less weirdness like jumping buses on a motorcycle or having a week of "congregational copulation" and more weirdness like praying for people's healing or casting out demonic forces. We believe some weird stuff! And keeping Christianity weird involves becoming all the more resolved to not only believe but also live out those beliefs.

Here are a few of the weird things we believe:

Believing in an ineffable God

To say God is ineffable is to mean God is too great, too awesome to ever be described in words. God is beyond our ability to define or express. In fact, Israel believed Yahweh was so ineffable that his name could not be even uttered, and in Exodus 33:20, God tells Moses, "You cannot see my face, for no one may see me and live."

It's quite common these days to speak of God as our friend, which in Christ he is, but we ought not lose the sense of awe, mystery, and otherness that is inherent to the way the Bible speaks about God. In Scripture, God is shown to be wholly distinct from creation. Of course, God is also shown as desiring and seeking out relationship with humankind, but we can't forget that God is above and beyond everything he has made. This is different from Hindu teaching, which emphasizes the divine presence *within* the universe. What we see in the world and the cosmos is a manifestation of the divine. Likewise, views such as pantheism (the belief that God and the universe are entirely one) and panentheism (the belief that while God is greater than the universe, that the universe is contained within God) are pretty popular these days. I sometimes even hear Christians speak of God in terms that sound like these views.

The God of the Bible is omnipresent, and may be experienced within time and space, but God exists apart from creation. In Isaiah 66:1-2, God says, "Heaven is my throne, and the earth is my footstool. Where is the house you will build for me? Where will my resting place be? Has not my hand made all these things, and so they came into being?" And in his prayer of dedication for the Temple he built in Jerusalem, King Solomon says, "But will God really dwell on earth? The heavens, even the highest heaven, cannot contain you. How much less this temple I have built!" (1 Kings 8:27).

In a day where people routinely talk about God providing them with parking spaces at the local mall, believing God is holy, ineffable, utterly free, and beyond our agendas is kind of weird. It reminds me of Christian Smith's research into the religious beliefs of American teenagers, published as *Soul Searching* in 2005. He claimed that American adolescents weren't so much Christian in their outlook (even when they self-identified as such), but could be better described as holding to what he termed "Moralistic Therapeutic Deism."

Smith described Moralistic Therapeutic Deism as consisting of the following beliefs:

- "A God exists who created and orders the world and watches over human life on earth."
- "God wants people to be good, nice, and fair to each other, as taught in the Bible and by most world religions."

- "The central goal of life is to be happy and to feel good about oneself."
- "God does not need to be particularly involved in one's life except when God is needed to resolve a problem."
- "Good people go to heaven when they die." (Or turn into angels, as the case may be.)[10]

It's so unchallenging. God is always on my side. I can call on him any time I like and he will come running. No wonder atheists mock us for believing in a "Magic Sky Daddy." In a world of Moralistic Therapeutic Deism, keeping Christianity weird involves recovering our strange belief in a scary God who can't ever be fully known, who doesn't need us, whose face we can't look upon, and whose name we can't utter.

Believing in the Incarnation

Having said all that, this scary God hasn't abandoned us. God loves us and has humbled, or limited, himself to take on flesh and dwell among us.[11] When you think about it, the Incarnation is the weirdest doctrine of all. No wonder Jews and Muslims consider our belief that Jesus is God in human form to be blasphemous, even repulsive. Jesus isn't just a godly man or a holy man. He isn't just a great teacher or a fine moral example. Jesus is God. Jesus is fully divine and fully human. That's as weird a belief as you can get.

You see, in Jewish religious practice, not only could God's name not be uttered, but it was strictly forbidden to create any visual representation of him, in any form (Deuteronomy 4:15-19). Jews were banned from fashioning sculptures, carvings, or images of God. That was what the polytheistic pagan religions did. Not Israel. God could never be contained or represented in physical form. So to say the Creator had squeezed himself into a human body, one that needed food and sleep and was subject to normal bodily functions—well, that was blasphemy of the worst kind.

Today, rather than watering it down or feeling embarrassed about it, we need to be all the more open about the Incarnation. It is the defining belief of the Christian faith. C. S. Lewis referred to the Incarnation as the central miracle of history. He was noted for having said that all miracles before the Incarnation point toward it, and all miracles since proceed from it.

Believing in the Resurrection

You might be familiar with Paul's presentation to the philosophers in the Areopagus in Athens. It's recorded in Acts 17, where we're told those who invited him had said, "May we know what this new teaching is that you are presenting? You are bringing some strange ideas to our ears, and we would like to know what they mean" (verses 19-20). The writer of Acts slips in a comment in parentheses that the city was inflamed with discussing "the latest ideas" (verse 21), so you'd think this was a happy hunting ground for Paul. He launches into one of his best-known presentations, beginning with some flattering comments about their commendable interest in religious ideas, before making a case for the existence of the Hebrew (monotheistic) God, and rounding off with a statement about Jesus, the coming judgment, and the Resurrection.

At that point, the party pretty much breaks up. The Epicurean and Stoic philosophers who had invited him to the forum to share his "strange ideas" roll their eyes and sneer derisively. Obviously, when they said they wanted to hear his strange ideas, they didn't mean *strange* ideas. It's Paul's mention of resurrection that does it. Apparently, believing a man could defeat death and return to judge the living and the dead was just too weird, even for them.

It's no less weird for many people today. They don't mind if Neo from *The Matrix* or Harry Potter defeats death. That's just fiction. But if you say you actually believe Jesus was God in human form and that he took our punishment, that he conquered evil, brought forgiveness and defeated death, and through his resurrection he has ushered in a new social and political order according to God's purposes, someone will say you might as well believe in the Flying Spaghetti Monster.

Recently, on Facebook, someone took the opportunity to let me know that I'm a fool for believing "that a cosmic Jewish zombie who is his own father can make you live forever if you symbolically eat his flesh and drink his blood, while telepathically telling him that you can accept him as your master, so that he can remove an evil force from your soul which is present in all humanity because a woman made out of one rib bone and a mound of dirt was tricked into eating fruit from a magical tree by a talking snake." That's not an original insult. He'd copied and pasted it. It's all over the Internet. I can't find the original author, but it's popularity only reinforces the derision you're likely to incur if you believe wyrd stuff like the Resurrection.

Believing in—and joining—the ongoing incarnating mission of God

A little earlier, I mentioned that it was prohibited in Jewish religious practice to create any image of God. But while the Jews believed God could not be depicted visually, they nonetheless held to the belief that the *nature* of God was visible in humankind. This idea is called the "imago Dei," the idea that women and men reflect the nature and being of their Creator. This idea appears very early in the Bible, in the Jewish creation stories, where God says, "'Let us make mankind in our image, in our likeness.' . . . So God created mankind in his own image, in the image of God he created them; male and female he created them" (Genesis 1:26-27).

This had huge implications for Jewish society. The belief that human beings are made in the image of God meant that practices common to many other nations and religions around them—human sacrifice, emasculation, ritual prostitution, and the like—were not practiced in Israel. Human bodies reflected the image of God and were not to be abused in this way. On the positive side, it also led to a recognition of the need to care for the widow and orphan and to practice hospitality to the outsider and the sojourner. In other words, in its canonical form, Judaism was coded as weird long before the Pharisees and other forces smoothed its edges and tamed its wildness.

But it has even greater implications for the weird people who follow Jesus. As I just mentioned, we believe God took on flesh and dwelt among us in the person of Jesus. But we also believe the life, ministry, suffering, death, and resurrection of Jesus don't just form the content of our belief system. We believe the unique event of the Incarnation has definite concrete significance for the way in which the church carries out its mission. In other words, we believe the ongoing incarnating mission of God happens through the followers of Jesus, patterned on his life, ministry, and suffering, and enabled by the continuing power of the Incarnation. And we, like the Jews and early Christians, believe the imago Dei infuses all human beings and that everyone is deserving of the dignity, kindness, and liberty God intended for us in the beginning.

Our devotion to the kind of values that Weird Cities dream about emerges not from our self-conscious interest in being unconventional or different. It derives from two core beliefs—the imago Dei and the Incarnation. Because we believe every human life carries the fingerprints of their Creator God, we are impelled to work for justice and reconciliation, to protect the environment, to create safe, beautiful, creative spaces where people can flourish and find life.

We believe we are dependent beings made with the need for relationship with others and with our Creator. Only our Creator is independent of the need for others. We assume that each human being has been given by God not only the ability to seek after their Creator but also a longing, acknowledged or unacknowledged, to be united in relationship with him. We believe our task in this world is to embrace discipleship and sustainability, health and justice, beauty and peace. Only the ongoing incarnating power of God could deliver such a grand and beautiful vision of life.

In 2009, Emily Scott, the pastor of St. Lydia's Lutheran Church in Brooklyn, launched "Dinner Church," a Sunday gathering that takes place at a table around a meal that the participants cook together. There are no pews, no organ or choir, no pulpit. Just a table. Community is formed as those who gather share food and themselves by exploring Scripture, singing, and praying together. The group is encouraged to share their stories, but particularly to focus on the story of Christ's dying and rising, and in being shaped by the story, to learn to identify the deaths and resurrections that need to occur in their lives. As soon as you arrive at St. Lydia's, you are given a job to help out with the preparation of the meal. This act of both cooking and storying together has created a beautiful atmosphere in which lonely New Yorkers wishing to dispel feelings of isolation feel included and honored.

This is such a simple, embodied, communal activity, but it was considered so weird, it became something of a nationwide sensation. Media outlets picked up the story. A strange little church in Brooklyn was bringing people together to eat and drink in Jesus' name, and this was considered newsworthy!

But when you think about it, dinner church shouldn't be considered so innovative or strange. It's the way Christians gathered for the first 300 years of our existence. In Acts 2, we're told, "They broke bread in their homes and ate together with glad and sincere hearts" (verse 46). In the same way, when Paul rebuked the Corinthian church for practicing discrimination in their public gatherings (1 Corinthians 11:17-34), it's clear he assumed their meetings would include a feast at which the Lord's Supper would be celebrated.

Early church fathers like Tertullian described these gatherings as "love feasts," celebrations of hospitality, worship, and communion around tables with food at the center. Indeed, critics of the early church were disturbed by these strange weekly gatherings of Christians. The Roman emperor Julian, deeply suspicious of the growing influence of the Christians in the fourth century, scoffed at what he referred to as "their so-called love-feast [open meals], or hospitality, or service of tables—for they have many ways of carrying it out and hence call it by many names."[12] It was his view that these meetings, open to all and full of great food, hospitality, and grace, were getting too popular. Julian was of the view that the Christians practiced dinner church in order to lead his citizens astray, like "those who entice children with a cake, and by throwing it to them two or three times induce them to follow them, and then, when they are far away from their friends cast them on board a ship and sell them as slaves."[13] In other words, the fourth-century version of dinner church was so delicious you couldn't keep people away!

And here was St. Lydia's garnering national media interest for doing what we probably should have been doing all along! As a result of those early stories about dinner church, soon other churches and groups of Christians started launching their own versions across the country. The dinner-church movement now boasts over one hundred table-based church gatherings. Kendall Vanderslice of Simple Church in Grafton, Massachusetts, says, "For contemporary dinner churches, returning to the table for worship aims to reclaim the social boundary-breaking power of the Eucharistic meal, signifying a commitment to unity in Christ's Body."[14]

In her article about the movement, Vanderslice quotes another member of Simple Church, saying,

> It feels natural. If you were to sit down at a table without a meal, you would feel like you were having a meeting, or like you were deliberating on something. The stakes would feel a little higher; people might feel a little more on edge. But eating, it reminds you of all the times you've eaten with friends before, or with family. It evokes a comfortable experience that I think allows people to be more real with each other.[15]

Rather than giving away AR-15 rifles for Father's Day or riding a wild horse in church, maybe we should be doing something *really* weird, like hosting a table full of neighbors sharing food and stories, learning Scripture, praying, giving, and serving. Maybe the image of the kind, gentle, intimate love of a dinner table full of guests is a weirder and truer picture of the church than we imagine. For those of us strange enough to believe in the Incarnation and the Resurrection and be convinced that the church is called to join the ongoing incarnating mission of God, the table is a more helpful symbol than the stadium or auditorium.

Keeping Christianity weird is no mean feat. There are powerful forces that work against godly weirdness. These cultural forces don't encourage our attachment to a sense of place or more socially and environmentally responsible consumption patterns. The prevailing cultural winds don't value such things as cultural and ethnic diversity or being open to the views of others. There are economic forces that care nothing for beautifying the built environment, or resisting gentrification, promoting boutique local industries, or addressing homelessness in more meaningful ways. We're discouraged from welcoming the outsider, practicing hospitality, feeding those in need, or listening to the views of all, especially the marginalized. It's only by continually returning to our weird theological beliefs and the strange example of

our king and friend, Jesus, that we can find the strength
and inspiration to continue the task of breaking with
convention and keeping Christianity weird.

As my friend Marcus Curnow prays,

> *In the beginning was the Word and the Word*
> *was God*
> *. . . and the Word became flesh and dwelt*
> *tabernacled,*
> *pitched the tent,*
> *moved into the neighborhood,*
> *hit the street,*
> *among us.*
> *God became a body! . . .*
> *I want you to be aware of your body*
> *Your butt sitting on the seat,*
> *Your dinner sitting at the bottom of your gut,*
> *Your mind full of the many thoughts of this day.*
> *You too are a body!*
> *But you are more than just body.*
> *More than "consumer."*
> *More than your appetites and your urges.*
> *May your body be charged, fired, infused with the*
> *power of the Holy Spirit.*
> *Like the saints of old may you [be] blessed with the*
> *knowledge of the profound connection between*
> *flesh and spirit.*

May you feel it in your body.

May you feel this connection when you eat.

May it be impossible for you to read the gospels
without getting hungry.

May you know what your food cost, not just what you
paid for it.

May it taste good!

May you feel this connection with the earth and
all creation,

May your hands and feet get dirty.

May you grow some good fruit.

May you feel this connection with others.

May you love your neighbour, not the ones you wish
you had but the ones you have; human and
creature!

May you be connected to community built on good sex
and intimate friendships.

May you know peace and reconciliation in the war
zones of relationship, family, household, church
and culture.

You are the body of Christ!

Christ has no body here on earth but yours!

Christ has no hands but yours.

Christ has no feet but yours.

Christ has no butt but yours!

So get it up off your seat.

> *Dwelt it, tabernacle it, pitch it, move it into the*
> *neighbourhood, hit the street with it.*
> *And may God the Creator, Redeemer and Sustainer of*
> *all bodies go with you.*
> *Amen*[16]

FOR YOUR CONSIDERATION

1. What is the zaniest thing you've ever seen a church do? What did you think of it then? What do you think of it now?

2. How does an awareness that you bear the image of God affect the way you practice your faith? How does the awareness that your neighbor bears the image of God affect your relationships?

3. How does the idea that you are called to join God's mission affect your way of practicing your faith?

4. What's one thing you can start doing to embrace the discipline of being different? What can you and your friends start doing to help keep Christianity weird?

NOTES

INTRODUCTION
1. Stanley Hauerwas, *Matthew*, Brazos Theological Commentary on the Bible (Grand Rapids: Brazos Press, 2006), 80.
2. Hauerwas, *Matthew*, 81.

CHAPTER 1: HERE'S TO THE CRAZY ONES
1. Rob Siltanen, "The Real Story behind Apple's 'Think Different' Campaign," *Forbes*, December 14, 2011, https://www.forbes.com /sites/onmarketing/2011/12/14/the-real-story-behind-apples-think -different-campaign/2/#31d25bd47e56.
2. "Think Different," Apple Computer, Inc., accessed January 24, 2018, http://www.thecrazyones.it/spot-en.html#.
3. Evan Wiggs, *Engines of Heaven: Secrets of the Supernatural Life* (Bloomington, IN: Xlibris, 2013), 182.
4. Michael J. Colacurcio, *Godly Letters: The Literature of the American Puritans* (Notre Dame, IN: University of Notre Dame Press, 2006), 409.
5. Richard Beck, "Eccentric Christianity: Part 1, A Peculiar People," *Experimental Theology* (blog), August 13, 2014, accessed April 6, 2017, http://experimentaltheology.blogspot.com.au/2014/08 /eccentric-christianity-part-1-peculiar.html.
6. Richard Beck, *Unclean: Meditations on Purity, Hospitality, and Mortality* (Cambridge, England: Lutterworth Press, 2012), 130.
7. Beck, "Eccentric Christianity: Part 1."

8. Michael Frost, *Surprise the World: The Five Habits of Highly Missional People* (Colorado Springs, CO: NavPress, 2016), 10.

9. Richard Beck, "Eccentric Christianity: Part 2, The Eccentric God, Transcendence and the Prophetic Imagination," *Experimental Theology* (blog), August 14, 2014, accessed April 6, 2017, http://experimentaltheology.blogspot.com.au/2014/08/eccentric-christianity-part-2-eccentric.html.

10. Beck, "Eccentric Christianity: Part 2."

11. Richard Beck, "Eccentric Christianity: Part 7, The Eccentric Kingdom," *Experimental Theology* (blog), August 26, 2014, accessed June 5, 2017, http://experimentaltheology.blogspot.com.au/2014/08/eccentric-christianity-part-7-eccentric.html.

12. Shelley Carson, "The Unleashed Mind: Why Creative People Are Eccentric," *Scientific American*, May 2011, accessed July 7, 2017, http://www.scientificamerican.com/article.cfm?id=the-unleashed-mind.

13. Carson, "The Unleashed Mind."

14. Carson, "The Unleashed Mind."

CHAPTER 2: WHAT ARE WEIRD CITIES TELLING US?

1. Clarisse Loughrey, "Here's What the Edward Scissorhands Suburb Looks Like 25 Years On," *Independent*, December 7, 2015, accessed July 7, 2017, http://www.independent.co.uk/arts-entertainment/films/news/heres-what-the-edward-scissorhands-suburb-looks-like-25-years-on-a6763486.html.

2. Kristian Fraga, ed., *Tim Burton: Interviews* (Jackson, MS: University Press of Mississippi, 2005), 35.

3. Chris DeWolf, "Why New Urbanism Fails," *Planetizen*, February 18, 2002, accessed July 10, 2017, http://www.planetizen.com/node/42.

4. DeWolf, "Why New Urbanism Fails."

5. Michael Sorkin, *Some Assembly Required* (Minneapolis: University of Minnesota Press, 2001), 65.

6. William Upski Wimsatt, "Five Myths About the Suburbs," *Washington Post*, February 11, 2011, accessed September 27, 2017, http://www.washingtonpost.com/wp-dyn/content/article/2011/02/11/AR2011021102615.html?utm_term=.3fb17a14dde4.

7. "Farmland," American Farmland Trust, accessed February 2, 2018, https://www.farmland.org/our-work/areas-of-focus/farmland.

8. I've written on this subject at my blog. See "What the Weird Cities Movement Is Showing the Suburban Church," March 14, 2017, http://mikefrost.net/weird-cities-movement-showing-suburban -church/.

9. This list is a summary of the characteristics explored in Joshua Long's PhD thesis. Joshua Long, "Weird City: Sense of Place and Creative Resistance in Austin, Texas" (PhD diss., University of Kansas, 2008), 218, https://kuscholarworks.ku.edu/bitstream /handle/1808/5250/umi-ku-2611_1.pdf;sequence=1.

10. Patrick Clark, "McMansions Define Ugly in a New Way: They're a Bad Investment," *Bloomberg*, August 23, 2016, https://www .bloomberg.com/news/articles/2016-08-23/mcmansions-define -ugly-in-a-new-way-they-re-a-bad-investment.

11. Ashley Lutz, "The American Suburbs As We Know Them Are Dying," *Business Insider*, March 5, 2017, https://amp-businessinsider-com.cdn .ampproject.org/c/s/amp.businessinsider.com/death-of-suburbia-series -overview-2017-3.

12. Lutz, "American Suburbs."

13. Lutz, "American Suburbs."

14. Lutz, "American Suburbs."

15. Ed Stetzer, *Planting Missional Churches: Your Guide to Starting Churches That Multiply* (Nashville: B&H Academic, 2016), 9.

16. Alan J. Roxburgh, *Reaching a New Generation: Strategies for Tomorrow's Church* (Vancouver: Regent College Publishing, 1993), 105.

17. Roxburgh, *Reaching a New Generation*.

18. Leo Hickman, "Just What Is It With Evangelical Christians and Global Warming?," *The Guardian*, April 17, 2009, https://www.theguardian .com/environment/blog/2009/apr/17/climate-change-religion.

19. Pew Research Center, "A Deeper Partisan Divide Over Global Warming," May 8, 2008, http://www.people-press.org/2008/05/08 /a-deeper-partisan-divide-over-global-warming/.

20. Scot McKnight, *A Fellowship of Differents: Showing the World God's Design for Life Together* (Grand Rapids: Zondervan, 2015), 17.

21. Stephen Tucker Paulsen, "The Depressing Truth About Hipster Food Towns," *Mother Jones*, Jan/Feb 2017, accessed August 1, 2017, http://www.motherjones.com/politics/2017/04/food-desert-mirage-gentrify-brooklyn-portland-groceries-snap.

CHAPTER 3: JESUS WAS THE ORIGINAL WEIRDO

1. Nick Cave, introduction to *The Gospel according to Mark* (Edinburgh: Canongate, 2010).

2. Cave, introduction to *Mark*.

3. Cave, introduction to *Mark*.

4. In saying this, I'm not suggesting that Jesus never referenced Old Testament examples. He defended his approach to the Sabbath by referring to David eating the show bread at the Tabernacle, and he quoted the Torah to the devil in the desert temptations. My point is that his homely examples weren't typical of the way Israel's religious leaders taught at the time.

5. See Malka Z. Simkovich, "Abraham as the Great (Un)Circumciser," TheTorah.com, accessed January 5, 2017, http://thetorah.com/abraham-circumcision/.

6. See endnote 5 of chapter 1.

7. James H. Cone, *A Black Theology of Liberation, Fortieth Anniversary Edition* (Maryknoll, NY: Orbis Books, 1986, 1990, 2010), ix..

8. Marvin R. Wilson, *Our Father Abraham: Jewish Roots of the Christian Faith* (Grand Rapids: William. B. Eerdmans, 1989), 117.

9. James L. Resseguie, *The Strange Gospel: Narrative Design and Point of View in John* (Lieden, Netherlands: Brill, 2001), 118.

CHAPTER 4: BEFORE WE BECAME CONVENTIONAL

1. Alan Kreider, *The Patient Ferment of the Early Church* (Grand Rapids, MI: Baker Academic, 2016), 1.

2. Kreider, *Patient Ferment*, 1–2.

3. Kreider, *Patient Ferment*, 183.

4. Kreider, *Patient Ferment*, 183.

5. "Alexander McQueen: Savage Beauty, May 4–August 7, 2011," The Metropolitan Museum of Art, accessed February 1, 2018, http://blog.metmuseum.org/alexandermcqueen/about/.

6. George G. Hunter III, *The Celtic Way of Evangelism: How Christianity Can Reach the West . . . AGAIN* (Nashville: Abingdon Press, 2010), 65.

7. Cornelius J. Dyck, *An Introduction to Mennonite History* (Scottdale, PA: Herald Press, 1967), 45.

8. Dan Graves, "Menno Simons, Fugitive Leader," Christianity.com, April 28, 2010, http://www.christianity.com/church/church-history /timeline/1201-1500/menno-simons-fugitive-leader-11629900.html.

9. Menno Simons, quoted in Ted Lewis, "True Evangelical Faith," *The Mennonite*, July 7, 2009, https://themennonite.org/feature/true -evangelical-faith/. Condensed from list form; wording retained.

10. Matthew Avery Sutton, *Amy Semple McPherson and the Resurrection of Christian America* (Cambridge: Harvard University Press, 2007), 28–29.

11. Sutton, *McPherson and the Resurrection*, 29.

12. Sutton, *McPherson and the Resurrection*, 36.

13. A. W. Tozer, *The Root of the Righteous* (Chicago: Moody Publishers, 1955, 1986), 189.

CHAPTER 5: WHAT KILLS THE WEIRD?

1. Richard Rohr, "Liminal Space," Center for Action and Contemplation, July 7, 2016, accessed March 30, 2017, https://cac.org/liminal-space -2016-07-07/.

2. Malcolm Gladwell, "The Big Man Can't Shoot," *Revisionist History*, podcast, Season 1, episode 3, https://medium.com/@emaina1/the-big -man-cant-shoot-with-malcolm-gladwell-revisionist-history-podcast -transcript-8c530302e964.

3. Gladwell, "Big Man."

4. Gladwell, "Big Man."

5. Gladwell, "Big Man."

6. Gladwell, "Big Man."

7. Amanda Smith, *An Autobiography: The Story of the Lord's Dealings with Mrs. Amanda Smith, the Colored Evangelist* (Chicago: Meyer & Brother, 1893), 197.

8. Smith, *An Autobiography*, 76–77, 79.

9. Smith, *An Autobiography*, 198.

CHAPTER 6: SEEING THINGS WEIRDLY

1. Stanley Hauerwas, *Matthew*, Brazos Theological Commentary on the Bible (Grand Rapids: Brazos Press, 2006), 67–68.

2. Hauerwas, *Matthew*, 67.

3. Hauerwas, *Matthew*, 67–68.

4. Harold Kushner, *Who Needs God* (New York: Fireside, 2002), 40.

5. Emily Badger and Niraj Chokshi, "How We Became Bitter Political Enemies," *New York Times*, June 15, 2017, https://www.nytimes.com /2017/06/15/upshot/how-we-became-bitter-political-enemies.html.

6. Bill Bishop, *The Big Sort: Why the Clustering of Like-Minded America Is Tearing Us Apart* (New York: Houghton Mifflin, 2008), 14.

7. Bishop, *The Big Sort*, 39.

8. Badger and Chokshi, "How We Became." Emphasis added.

9. Badger and Chokshi, "How We Became."

10. I've written at greater length on this topic at my blog. See "We Don't Need a More Violent Christianity (It's Plenty Violent Already)," June 1, 2017, http://mikefrost.net/dont-need-violent-christianity -plenty-violent-already/.

11. All Daubenmire quotes here are found at Ed Brayton, "'Coach' Dave Wants a 'More Violent Christianity,'" *Patheos*, May 30, 2017, http://www.patheos.com/blogs/dispatches/2017/05/30/coach-dave -wants-violent-christianity/.

12. Hauerwas, *Matthew*, 67.

13. Tim Soerens and Christiana Rice, "5 Hopeful Signs that Dare Us to Be the Church," *ChristianWeek*, April 19, 2016, http://www .christianweek.org/5-hopeful-signs-dare-us-church/.

14. Soerens and Rice, "5 Hopeful Signs."

15. Soerens and Rice, "5 Hopeful Signs."

16. Giles Fraser, "After the Grenfell Fire, the Church Got It Right Where the Council Failed," *The Guardian*, June 22, 2017, https:// www.theguardian.com/commentisfree/belief/2017/jun/22/after-the -grenfell-fire-the-church-got-it-right-where-the-council-failed.

17. Fraser, "After the Grenfell Fire."

18. N. T. Wright, *Surprised by Hope: Rethinking Heaven, the Resurrection, and the Mission of the Church* (New York: HarperOne, 2008), 265–66.

19. Fraser, "After the Grenfell Fire."

CHAPTER 7: IF WE'RE NOT WEIRD, WE'RE DOING IT WRONG

1. "Pastor Parsley Zip-Lines to Pulpit over Cheering Congregants," *Stand Up for the Truth*, March 25, 2013, https://standupforthetruth .com/2013/03/pastor-parsley-zip-lines-to-pulpit-over-cheering -congregants/.

2. Morgan Lee, "Pastor Rides Wild Horse into Converted Rodeo Arena Sanctuary as Part of Sermon Illustration," *Christian Post*, December 9, 2013, https://www.christianpost.com/news/pastor -rides-wild-horse-into-converted-rodeo-arena-sanctuary-as-part-of -sermon-illustration-110383/.

3. Frank Heinz, "Congregation Puts Pastor in Glass House," NBCDFW.com, April 27, 2009, https://www.nbcdfw.com/news /weird/Congregation-Puts-Pastor-in-a-Box.html.

4. "Jumping for the King: Preacher to Jump over Nine Buses, Wall of Fire," *Dangerous Minds*, April 5, 2011, https://dangerousminds.net /comments/jumping_for_the_king_preacher_to_jump_over_nine _buses_wall_of_fire.

5. David Gibson, "Top 12 Pastor Stunts: Living as an Atheist Is Just the Latest Ministry Gimmick," *St. Louis Post-Dispatch*, January 17, 2014, http://www.stltoday.com/lifestyles/faith-and-values/top -pastor-stunts-living-as-an-atheist-is-just-the/article_c048bc0e-2f92 -5873-a3b3-23cf28f50b81.html.

6. Lee Moran, "Missouri Church Gives Away Assault Rifles to Get More Young Men Following Jesus," *New York Daily News*, June 23, 2014, http://www.nydailynews.com/news/national/mo-church -assault-rifles-young-men-jesus-article-1.1840066.

7. Seth Tower Hurd, "Do Church 'Publicity Stunts' Send the Wrong Message?," *Relevant*, October 9, 2014, www.relevantmagazine.com /god/church/do-church-publicity-stunts-send-wrong-message.

8. "Obama Decries Quran-Burning, Violent Responses," CNN.com, April 2, 2011, http://www.cnn.com/2011/WORLD/asiapcf/04/02 /afghanistan.pastor.protest/index.html.

9. Chris Higgins, "Brian Kidd Is the Unipiper: The Unicycling Bagpiper," *Boingboing*, January 6, 2014, https://boingboing.net/2014/01/06/the -unipiper.html.

10. Christian Smith, *Soul Searching: The Religious and Spiritual Lives of American Teenagers* (Oxford: Oxford University Press, 2005), 162–63.

11. See John 1:14.

12. John Dickson, *The Best Kept Secret of Christian Mission: Promoting the Gospel with More than Our Lips* (Grand Rapids, MI: Zondervan, 2010), 93.

13. Dickson, *Best Kept Secret*, 93.

14. Kendall Vanderslice, "Dinner Churches Spring Up Nationwide," Christian Food Movement, January 13, 2017, http://christian foodmovement.org/2017/01/13/dinner-churches-spring-up -nationwide/.

15. Vanderslice, "Dinner Churches."

16. Marcus Curnow, "Incarnation Benediction," unpublished, used with permission. See https://marcuscurnow.wordpress.com/2005 /02/25/benediction-incarnation-forge/.

Change Your Habits, Change Your World

Take your friends, your small group, even your church on a journey. The five habits in *Surprise the World* will help you live out your faith together in ways that draw others to Christ.